To Stephen,
may God bless you
always!
Father Bob Lauder

MAGNETIZED BY GOD

Religious Encounters
through Film, Theater,
Literature and Painting

MAGNETIZED BY GOD
Religious Encounters through Film, Theater, Literature and Painting

Rev. Robert E. Lauder

Resurrection Press
An Imprint of
CATHOLIC BOOK PUBLISHING CO.
Totowa • New Jersey

Grateful acknowledgment is made to the Long Island Catholic for material which originally appeared in its pages.

First published in September, 2004 by
Catholic Book Publishing/Resurrection Press
77 West End Road
Totowa, NJ 07512

ISBN 1-878718-92-4
Library of Congress Catalog Card Number: 2004106631

Cover design by Beth DeNapoli

Printed in the United States of America

1 2 3 4 5 6 7 8 9

Dedication

To Zachary with prayers, love and hope
and to Alysoun Roach and Robert Abiuso
with much gratitude for their friendship.

Contents

Foreword

IT has been four decades since the the Vatican Council issued the great document *Gaudium et Spes.* It signaled the Church's willingness to be open to the modern world and the end of the now weary battle between the Church and the Enlightenment. Those who would like to restore the Church to the condition it was in before the Council take particular umbrage towards "Joy and Hope." They either denounce it as influenced by the Enlightenment a pre-Council shibboleth or chortle that "modernism" has been replaced by "post-modernism" —as though anyone knows what post-modernism is besides an intellectual fad.

Such men who wish to nitpick away the Council will in due course be swept away into the ash cans of history. Yet their ascendancy in the Church is evidence that the gloom which the Council tried to sweep away has reasserted itself. In a garrison under assault one must see the world as godless, sinful, ugly, evil, the kind of place which the Church and Catholics must avoid, even perhaps hide from out in the desert.

It may be questionable whether such a project is feasible any more save for the few who have an eremitic vocation. It is also questionable whether any age in human history would not appear as equally evil. Finally, it is questionable whether there were not churchmen in every age who were similar prophets of doom. However, these men were soon forgotten. At its best the Church tried to absorb everything that was good, true, and beautiful in its environment – Roman law, corporate structure, and architecture, Greek and Jewish music, Greek philosophy (actually twice, the second time as transmitted by Arabs), Anglo Saxon Spring festivals, Irish poetry and art, vernacular literature and music—the list could fill many pages of proof that the Church at its best is not afraid of the modern world, whatever modern is.

Nonetheless, despite *Gaudium et Spes*, the atmosphere in the Church today is not sympathetic to the efforts of men like Father Lauder who try to find in contemporary literature, film, and art magnets hidden by an ingenious God to attract us. Despite Pope John Paul II's Easter Letter to artists, such attempts to find enchanting beauty in the culture around us are viewed as something that some people do, but not a program for revivifying Catholicism. If Father Lauder wants to spend time with Eugene O'Neill, Flannery O'Connor, Alice McDermott, Woody Allen, and surrealistic painting, well, that's all right, we suppose, but might not the time be better spent feeding the poor or fighting against abortion.

This is a terrible position for a Church which produced Chartres, the *Divine Comedy*, Don Quixote, and the "May Magnificat." In the present time of chaos and conflict all we have left is Beauty. That is enough, however, because if we can enchant people with Beauty we then can attract them to goodness and truth. The Church has no monopoly on beauty, though it has certainly created enough of it through the ages. However, its great strength is that it has a fine eye for beauty wherever it may be found and eagerly pursues it and makes it its own. Father Lauder merely continues that quest to find beauty and Beauty's God wherever it may lurk.

I am convinced that when the Church pulls itself out of the mess that both the left and the right have created, it will do so because it has recaptured its passion for beauty as a sacrament of God.

Andrew Greeley
Eastertide 2004

Introduction

"… there is no secular realm, if by 'secular' we mean 'ungraced'" [1]
—Michael Himes

IT is interesting to me how a book gets born. This one started with a title that I liked. While writing it I discovered it involved reflecting on what is most important in my life. I believe that every person is "magnetized by God," drawn by God, for a loving eternal union with God. As I reflected on my own journey, I became aware what a large role art has played and is playing in my life. Reading the truly magnificent letter of Pope John Paul II to Artists (1999), I was moved to write this book. The Holy Father's statements about art and artists removed any residual doubts I might have had about the relevance or importance of reflecting in print on the value of art and its special role in helping people grow in wisdom and grace.

The Holy Father dedicated his letter in the following way: "To all who are passionately dedicated to the search for new 'epiphanies' of beauty so that through their creative work as artists they may offer these as gifts to the world."

In my life I have received many gifts from artists, "epiphanies" that have greatly enriched my life. In recent years I have become increasingly appreciative of those "epiphanies," more grateful for the gifts artists have given me and so this book is a kind of "thank you." I write about art and its revelation of God drawing us into relationships in the hope that I can share what I received with others. The book is not a scholarly comprehensive discussion of art. It is anecdotal and autobiographical. Art, especially film, theater, literature and painting have helped me see the face of God and the presence of God in my fellow sojourners and in myself. Hoping that my experience of art and the special meanings and mysteries it reveals might speak to others, I offer this book.

In his letter Pope John Pope II comments on how artists imitate God:

"God therefore called man into existence, committing to him the craftsman's task. Through his 'artistic creativity' man appears more than ever 'in the image of God,' and he accomplishes this task above all in shaping the wondrous 'material' of his own humanity and then exercising creative dominion over the universe which surrounds him. With loving regard, the divine Artist passes on to the human artist a spark of his own surpassing wisdom, calling him to share in his creative power.

"Not all are called to be artists in the specific sense of the term. Yet, as Genesis has it, all men and women are entrusted with the task of crafting their own life: in a certain sense, they are to make of it a work of art, a masterpiece."[2]

The sparks of the Divine that artists give off can help the rest of us craft our lives into the masterpieces that God has called us to be.

Any part of reality can become sacramental for us. Theologian Father Michael Himes makes this point well in his book *Doing the Truth in Love: Conversations about God, Relationships and Service.* Commenting on grace, which is theological shorthand for God's loving presence in our lives, Father Himes writes:

> "So grace is everywhere. This claim has very important consequences. Often we speak of the sacred as though it was a quite separate realm from the secular. What I am suggesting is that there is no secular realm, if by 'secular' we mean 'ungraced' or 'unrelated' to the *'agape'* of God. There may be many aspects of life about which we do not customarily use religious or theological language to talk about our experience, but that does not mean that those realms of experience are ungraced. Every aspect of our being is ultimately connected to the fundamental question of where we stand in face of the *'agape'* of God." [3]

By the *'agape'* of God Father Himes means God's self-gift to the human race. That gift comes to us in many ways. Film, theater, literature and painting can be God's channels. They can provide opportunities for us to encounter God. The loving presence of God in our lives is like a magnet drawing us into a love relationship with Love Itself.

Questions for Reflection

1. According to John Paul II why are artists like God?
2. What does the author mean by grace? By *agape*?

[1] Michael Himes, *Doing The Truth in Love: Conversations About God, Relationship and Service* (New York: Paulist Press, 1995), p. 103.

[2] Pope John Paul II, *Letter to Artists* (April 4, 1999) Online Edition—Vol. V, No. 5: July—August, 1999, p.2.

[3] Michael Himes, *op. cit.*, pp. 103-104.

1

The Meaning of Art

"... people seek an absolute ... a final explanation ..." [1]
—Pope John Paul II

The Importance of Truth

One of the ways that important meanings and profound truths reach us is through art. Great films, theater, literature and painting can reveal to us who we are. They can tell us truths that we either never knew or have forgotten. They can call us to pause and reflect deeply on what should matter most in our lives. They can serve as messages from God.

I tend to be a very active person, involved in many apostolates. I seem to be always racing somewhere or preoccupied with some future activity. What I have noticed during the last few years is that I no sooner finish with one project than I am on to another, not even pausing to enjoy whatever success or fulfillment the first project provided. I frequently experience pressure, most of it self-inflicted.

I believe that God dwells within me at the deepest level of myself. I know that God wants me to enter into a deep love relationship. God is embracing me. This belief gives me great joy. I want to carry this belief into my daily life, to allow anxiety to pass, to live my belief that God is in the present. All of us should embrace the God Who is embracing us. The most important meaning in our lives should be that God is totally in love with us. Somehow that most important meaning and other important meanings can be missed.

If there is one thing that every college professor agrees with, it is that most contemporary students tend to be relativists. Was this tendency prevalent when I was an undergraduate 50 years ago? I doubt it. I first noticed the tendency toward relativism about 25 years ago when I was teaching part-time at a secular college. The basic attitude of the students was that no one knew what was the truth, that no one could be sure that he or she had discovered truth and that to suggest that there just might be some type of "absolute truth" was undemocratic, un-American and a sign of pride. The general attitude was that something might be truth for one person but not for another and to claim that a view held by someone else was false made you guilty of the worst kind of snobbery. It seemed to imply that you thought of yourself as better than the person whom you considered to be in error.

I now find relativism quite widespread among college students who are studying philosophy. It takes a considerable amount of time to dissuade them, but it is time well spent. If we do not believe that there is absolute truth, then of course we will not search for it or be ready to treasure it if we find it. In fact there is no reality more important for people than truth, except love. Pope John Paul II in a recent encyclical "Faith and Reason" stresses the danger of relativism. Pointing out that right now there is a widespread philosophical skepticism, the Holy Father writes:

"... Everything is reduced to opinion; and there is a sense of being adrift. While on the one hand philosophical thinking has succeeded in coming closer to the reality of human life and its forms of expression, it has also tended to pursue issues – existential, hermeneutical or linguistic – which ignore the radical question of the truth about personal existence, about being and about God. Hence we see among the men and women of our time, and not just in some philosophers, attitudes of widespread distrust of the human being's great capacity for knowledge. With a false modesty, people rest content with partial and provisional truths, no longer seeking to ask radical questions about the meaning and ultimate foundation of human, personal and social existence. In short, the hope that philosophy might be able to provide definitive answers to these questions has dwindled."[2]

The pope has articulated an enormous problem in the contemporary world. Probably his words have special power for me because at the time I was reading the encyclical I was struggling with people, both students and others, to help them see that truth, especially profound truth about ourselves, our neighbors and God, though difficult to reach, is attainable.

At St. John's University in New York, where I teach philosophy, when the students and I reach the part of a course in which we are discussing questions about the nature of truth, about whether we can reach truth, about whether we can be certain that we have reached the truth, about whether there is absolute truth, I do everything short of standing on my head to impress them with the significance of what we are doing. At the University, every student must take at least three courses in philosophy but there are colleges and universities in this country in which students need not take any philosophy courses. I find this almost unbelievable. Every year people who have never seriously studied the nature of truth receive college diplomas. How can they be considered educated?

Pursuing truth is one of the activities that distinguishes us from the rest of God's creatures. I try to impress on students at St. John's that studying philosophy at one of the largest, if not the largest, Catholic university in the country can be a tremendous blessing. They have the opportunity to struggle with the most important questions that human beings have ever asked and the opportunity to discover some answers. Unfortunately, many students and others tend to think of philosophy as an ivory tower activity, an impractical reflection on abstract topics. The pope's encyclical, "Faith and Reason," can serve as a powerful correction of that misunderstanding. There is a sense in which nothing is more powerful than truth. Error does not make us free but rather hinders our personal growth. Truth about ourselves, our neighbors and God can free us and can enable us to grow as persons. The pope sees that deeply and in his encyclical he has tried to communicate his own reverence and enthusiasm for truth to us.

While reading the encyclical "Faith and Reason," I made note of certain passages which I found either especially illuminating or important. I came upon one that made me think of many contemporary artists whose work I admire but who seem unable to affirm what I consider to be the most important truths about the human person. In the section of the encyclical to which I am referring the pope mentions that truth comes initially to the human being as a question. We want to know if life has a meaning and where human life is going, if it is going anywhere. The pope points out that the first absolutely certain truth of our life, beyond the fact of our own existence, is our death. The search for an answer is inescapable. The Holy Father goes on to say that each of us has both the desire and the duty to know the truth about our destiny. Why are we here and where are we going? We want to know if death is the end or if we can hope for life beyond the grave. The pope writes:

"No one can avoid this questioning, neither the philosopher nor the ordinary person. The answer we give will determine whether or not we think it possible to attain universal and absolute truth; and this is a decisive moment of the search. Every truth – if it really is truth – presents itself as universal, even if it is not the whole truth. If something is true, then it must be true for all people and at all times. Beyond this universality, however, people seek an absolute which might give to all their searching meaning and an answer – something ultimate, which might serve as the ground of all things. In other words, they seek a final explanation, a supreme value... Hypotheses may fascinate, but they do not satisfy. Whether we admit it or not, there comes for everyone the moment when personal existence must be anchored to a truth recognized as final, a truth which confers a certitude no longer open to doubt."[3]

I agree with what the Holy Father has written but unfortunately a culture can distract people from the basic questions, from the topics that have preoccupied philosophers. The search that every person is called to engage in can be made to seem irrelevant. A culture can stunt our desire for truth. I find some of my contemporaries unable to reflect on serious questions, unable to think deeply about what is most important in their lives. I think that the culture does not call them to deep reflection or serious self-examination.

What ought to be happening in a philosophy classroom in a formal way is the kind of questioning and searching that some people, who have never taken a course in philosophy, engage in frequently. Rather than dealing with topics and questions that are esoteric and only real for academics, philosophy in a classroom ought to be dealing with matters of life and death, matters of ultimate importance, questions that are unavoidable for the reflective person.

Divine Revelation and Faith

Over the last few years I think that I have deepened my understanding of what divine revelation and faith are. I like the definitions of divine revelation and faith offered

by Edmond J. Dunn in his book *What Is Theology?* I confess that for much of my life I thought of divine revelation
as a set of answers that God sent down from heaven to us.
I almost thought of it as a kind of special catechism. When
as a seminarian, I studied theology, I may have thought of
divine revelation as a theology book with special propositions that God has sent us so that we can speak truthfully
about God. Faith, I thought, was a gift from God that
enabled us to believe those propositions that God had
sent. Looking back on my understanding of divine revelation, I think that my view was very narrow and excessively intellectual. This is the definition of divine revelation that Father Dunn offers:

"God's gracious self-disclosure reaching out
to humans as an invitation (as well as promise) to
participate in God's own life of unfathomable
love, mediated to us through persons, nature,
history, everyday experience, and in an ultimate
way, in and through God's very Word, Jesus
Christ."[4]

I like everything about Dunn's definition. God speaks
to us, reveals Himself to us by inviting us to enter into
God's own personal life. That life of God is love beyond
our understanding but we are invited to share in it. No
matter how long we think about this or meditate on it,
why God would make such an invitation to us will
remain a mystery. Why would the God Who holds the
galaxies in existence, Who created all of reality from nothing, want me to be part of His inner life? That God should
want this is mind-boggling to me. The only answer that
we can come up with is that God loves us beyond our

ability to understand. God is making the offer to us constantly in our everyday lives. That means the offer can come to us through art, through film, theater, literature and painting. This offer comes to us through persons, nature, history and everyday experience. The offer especially comes through God's Son, Jesus Christ. Divine revelation does not just address my mind; it addresses me. God does not merely wish to inform me; God wishes to have a love relationship with me.

What is faith? This is Father Dunn's definition of faith:

"Faith is our freely given, graced response to God's invitation to a loving relationship that begins in preconceptual form but takes its cognitive form in creeds, preaching, prayer, doctrines, and dogmas of the faith community, and calls us to a discipleship of worship, personal transformation and action on behalf of justice." [5]

Faith is our response but we can only make the response because of God's grace. Faith is saying "Yes" to God's offer of friendship. In that sense faith is thanking God for the offer. A genuine sincere "Thank you" is saying yes to the person being thanked. Faith is a special kind of "Thank you." The dogmas of our faith and the creeds that we profess come from the community's love relationship with God. Dogmas and creeds are about the God Who loves us and in creeds we express that we have accepted God's offer of love. Our faith can grow because we can always say "Yes" more profoundly and we can always say "Thank you" more sincerely.

Nobody is able to respond to God without the help of the Holy Spirit. Our decision to accept God's invitation is our free decision but that decision is made possible by the loving presence of the Holy Spirit in our lives. Especially important for those of us who identify ourselves as believers is the point that faith "begins in the preconceptual form." First, the loving relationship between us and God takes place and then the creed, doctrines and dogmas. I believe that there are people who have freely accepted God's invitation and are close to God but they never get past the preconceptual level. Their faith never blossoms into creeds, doctrines or dogmas. In fact, if some of these people were asked if they believe in Christ they might answer negatively. What I am thinking of are the people who might have what theologians at one time called "baptism of desire." By that term they meant people who were of good will but for some reason could not consciously accept Christ. People who have "baptism of desire" may be very close to God and, if they knew God's will for them, they would do it. Whatever terminology theologians come up with, the key point is that there seem to be people who have a loving relationship with God but whose faith has not developed into Christian creeds, doctrines and dogmas. This is very encouraging. It reminds us that the Holy Spirit does not rely completely on our efforts and that the Holy Spirit is operative in ways we do not know.

Why does someone's faith stay at the preconceptual level? There could be many reasons. Perhaps the person's family was not religious and so the person's upbringing was irreligious; perhaps the person's education was greatly influenced by secular humanism; perhaps the public image of the Christian church is unattractive; perhaps the individual Christians that the person knows are at best unimpressive, and at worst religiously unattractive. There could be many other reasons.

I am thinking of a friend who I believe is very close to God but this person does not publicly express any faith. In conversations that I have had with my friend the most that she will say is "There is a mystery to life." I think that what she is calling mystery is what I call God. This person is very unselfish and very dedicated to helping people. She works very long hours trying to help people. She will say "Aren't I foolish? Why am I doing this? Why am I spending so much time working?" She does not know why. I think I know why. She is working so hard to help people because the Holy Spirit is moving her to do that. She is responding to the Holy Spirit's loving presence in her life. Of course, there is no way that I can prove that anymore than I can prove that something I do that seems like a good act is done because of the Holy Spirit's presence in my life. That there may be many people, who have accepted God's invitation to enter into a loving relationship but whose faith is still at the preconceptual level, should encourage us. God's love may be touching many people who do not seem to be religious believers.

The last part of Dunn's definition is important, that faith calls us to a "discipleship of worship, personal transformation, and action on behalf of justice." Each of these reminds me that faith is not merely an intellectual response but a personal response. My faith is not something that only *my mind* does but that *I do*. My response to God calls me to prayer, especially to the Eucharist. The Eucharist is *the* action of Catholic faith. In the Eucharistic liturgy, everything I believe as a Catholic is expressed, and

God's loving presence to me is especially evident. The Eucharist reviews the history of salvation and invites us, through participation in the Eucharist and through action that springs from the Eucharistic action, to become more consciously involved in the history of salvation. If a Catholic claims to believe in Christ but does not regularly attend the Eucharist, I wonder about that person's faith. What actually would that person's faith mean? What form would it take? What shape would it have? How would it be incarnated in that person's life? I am not judging anyone but the connection between Eucharist and a Catholic's faith seems obvious to me, indeed essential.

Our faith calls us to personal transformation. The loving relationship that we have with God calls us to live out that relationship in our daily lives. Our acceptance of God's invitation is the first step on a lifelong journey, a lifelong adventure. Everyone's life is supposed to be an adventure in grace. Our faith is not supposed to be like a Sunday set of clothes but rather a reality that permeates everything that we do. Decisions we make about vocations, jobs and marriage partners should not be divorced from our faith. Rather our faith should illuminate our lives and color our decisions. Faith ought to lead to action. We ought to remember that God's invitation, God's offer, is coming to us through many experiences.

I suppose that one of the most important aspects about faith is that, even though we have said "Yes" to God's invitation to enter into God's unfathomable life of love, we have a lifetime to keep saying "Yes." Because my faith is not strong today does not mean that it cannot be stronger tomorrow. There is a Holy Spirit, the Spirit of

Love, encouraging us and inspiring us and aiding us. Perhaps part of our faith life is being patient with ourselves. God is patient and perhaps we can imitate that patience. God's gifts surround us, and we will never appreciate them sufficiently. Someone has said that God's gifts put our greatest dreams and desires to shame. One of the greatest of these gifts is faith.

Listening to Art

In his book *The Good Listener*[6], Father James Sullivan provides excellent insights into the art of listening. Though it can seem like such a simple activity, listening is extremely important in interpersonal relationships. I believe that we have to learn to be listeners. To really listen requires more than having two ears that function properly. It requires a special kind of presence to another person, an openness, a readiness to receive. If I listen attentively to another person, then I am focusing in on how the person is revealing himself or herself. In real conversation gifts are exchanged. Persons, when they speak seriously, say who they are. Their words reveal themselves. Human speech at its best is self-revelatory. Listening is not only beneficial to the person who is listened to but also beneficial to the listener. Becoming a good listener is becoming a better person, psychologically, morally and spiritually.

As I am writing this I am thinking of some of my friends. Several of them are marvelous listeners. When I speak about something important to them I can actually observe them focusing their attention on me. They become present in a special way. I love to talk to them because I know that they care about me and are listening to me. Their very act of listening attentively and lovingly is helpful, no matter what the words they speak.

I believe that a human life has a unity to it. To talk about my spiritual life or my emotional life or my religious life may be necessary in order to help me understand myself better, but the danger is that I will compartmentalize the various aspects of my life and come to think that each part of my life is somehow separate from the others. Actually I don't have a spiritual life that is somehow separate from the other parts of my life. Though there are aspects and dimensions to my life, there is just one life that Robert Lauder is living. We want to listen for God's revelation, for God's self-gift. This takes place chiefly through the life, death and resurrection of God's Son. But God's revelation can be mediated in many ways. One mediator can be art and so we want to try to listen to art not just with our ears but as persons attentive and eager to receive. I have found film, theater, literature and painting wonderful mediators of God's revelation. If we listen carefully our faith may be nourished.

One day in a class at St. John's University, I was trying to explain how a story can grab our attention, can call us to listen. There were about 65 students in the classroom. In trying to impress on them how powerful a story can be, I decided to relate an experience I had in giving a homily. The students reacted exactly the same way that the members of the congregation did. During the homily, in order to illustrate a "death-bed-conversion," I told the story of the film, *Angels with Dirty Faces*, starring James Cagney and Pat O'Brien. In the film Cagney plays a killer, Rocky

Sullivan, and O'Brien plays his boyhood pal, Jerry Connolly, who has become a priest. Visiting Cagney just before the killer walks the "last mile" to the electric chair, O'Brien pleads with him to act as though he is afraid to die so that the teenagers who admire him so much will be revolted by his "cowardice." Telling Cagney that he wants him to straighten himself out with God, O'Brien realizes that he is asking a great deal. Cagney refuses, claiming that all he has left is his reputation as a tough guy. O'Brien is asking him to give up everything. With that great Cagney swagger, the killer walks toward the electric chair, but just as he enters the death chamber, he starts pleading, crying and whining that he does not want to die. It is a tremendous scene and a terrific image of someone meeting God at the last minute before death. For the sake of others, the killer gives up all he has left—his reputation as fearless—and acts as though he is a coward.

In the church, during my telling of the story, there was a hushed silence. There was the same silence in the St. John's classroom as I retold it. Stories really can grab people. If we "listen" to art we may hear God's voice.

Questions for Reflection

1. What does relativism say about truth?
2. How does relativism influence contemporary people's search for truth according to John Paul II?
3. What type of questioning cannot be avoided by anyone according to John Paul II?
4. How do you think of Divine Revelation? What is it? How do you think of faith? What is it?

5. What does theologian Edmond J. Dunn mean when he claims that faith begins "in pre-conceptual form"?

6. Do you think many people have what some theologians call "baptism of desire"?

7. Why does faith call us to personal transformation?

8. Do you "listen" to art? Can you give some examples of your experience of "listening" to art?

---

[1] John Paul II, *Faith and Reason* (Encyclical letter), September 14, 1998, Online Edition, p. 17.

[2] *Ibid.*, pp. 4-5.

[3] *Ibid.*

[4] Father Edmond J. Dunn, *What is Theology?* (Mystic, Connecticut: Twenty Third Publications, 1998), p. 42.

[5] Ibid., p. 53.

[6] Father James Sullivan, *The Good Listener* (Notre Dame, Indiana: Ave Maria Press, 2000), p.128.

2

The Mystery of Movies

"Some people think the crucifixion only took place on Calvary. They better wise up . . . "
—Karl Malden as Fr. Barry in *On The Waterfront*

The relationship between religion and film is important. I certainly do not want to equate religious practice with artistic or aesthetic experience, but I also do not want to distance them from one another either. What I want to do is distinguish them but not separate them.

Film that appeals to the lowest in us, that is pornographic in its depiction of sex and violence, obviously does not foster religious experience. Nor does film that has little insight into human nature, that presents a shallow or even erroneous view of human nature, ordinarily foster religious experience. However, I don't want to oversimplify. Film that presents a false view of human nature can be done so well that, because of its beauty, honesty and integrity, it indirectly fosters religious experience. I think of director William Wyler's *The Heiress* which seems to present vengeance as a way of growing toward personal freedom. The film is done so well that it might lead to reflection on the meaning of forgiveness and how that could lead to personal freedom and relationship with a forgiving God. The beauty, honesty and integrity of a film, even if its vision of reality is flawed, can mirror the beauty of God. In his letter to artists Pope John Paul II stated:

> "Every genuine art form in its own way is a path to the inmost reality of man and of the world. It is therefore a wholly valid approach to the realm of faith, which gives human experience its ultimate meaning. That is why the Gospel fullness of truth was bound from the beginning to stir the interest of artists, who by their very nature are alert to every 'epiphany' of the inner beauty of things." [1]

Much of contemporary film is in a sorry state. There is the obvious problem of too much violence and a very casual view of sexuality. However, another serious problem is that so much of contemporary film is dumb and seems to be getting dumber. A diet of this type of film can be a disaster in terms of religious experience. Dumb cinema drags us down. I suspect that some high school and college students have become incapable of watching a serious film. Their capacity to follow and appreciate a serious drama has been weakened by the awful films and television that they have seen. Even some who can follow such a film find it so demanding that it has little or no appeal to them.

Great film can foster religious experience. It would be wonderful if we had brilliant films that dramatize a human person's relationship with God. Occasionally we do encounter such works or art, but to have them as a regular experience would almost require that something like the Judeo-Christian vision permeated society and nourished artists. That is not the contemporary situation.

Though we do not have many films that deal directly and specifically with religious experience, we do have some great films that see so deeply into human nature and provide such a spiritual experience that they indirectly foster religious experience. This is where the education of religious believers is crucial. We don't have to try to "baptize" every film and try to say that the work is saying all sorts of things which it does not say and which the artist never intended the work to say. However, I do believe that we can view a film with religious faith and see meanings about life and human persons which someone without faith might miss. What I am imagining is that the work of art is so profound that it allows us to link its themes with what we believe about God and the human person. Great films may not directly provide religious experience, but they can provide insights that reveal the mystery of life and indirectly aid us in our journey toward God.

Two examples from my own experience may make my position more clear. I cannot view Elia Kazan's *On the Waterfront,* which is my favorite film, without wanting to be a better priest. The film always moves me deeply, reminds me of God's love for us and inspires me to reach out and help others. I cannot view Frank Capra's *It's a Wonderful Life* without being grateful for my friends and wanting to be a better person. Both of these films are outstanding works of art that reveal the human mystery and, I believe, the mystery of God to us in a very powerful way. Because of that they can make the world of faith more real to us and can foster religious experience.

Just about everything in *On the Waterfront* works beautifully. The script, acting, music, editing and direction combine to make an American classic. The artists involved with the film hit their peak in this work. Marlon Brando as Terry Malloy, the longshoreman ex-boxer converted through the presence of Edie (Eva Marie Saint) and Father Barry (Karl Malden) in his life turns in the performance of a lifetime. Saint and Malden never topped their performances and Lee J. Cobb is excellent as Johnny Friendly the gangster who controls the union. Leonard Bernstein's music is magnificent and Kazan weaves all the artistic contributions into a masterpiece.

The film contains one of the great religious speeches in the history of cinema. Father Barry had made a promise to "K.O." Dugan (Pat Henning) that if Dugan stuck his neck out by testifying before the Waterfront Crime Commission and told what he knew about corruption on the waterfront, Father Barry would not stop battling corruption even if Dugan was murdered. Standing in the hull of a ship next to the body of the murdered Dugan, which he has just anointed, Father Barry keeps his promise. The following are excerpts from his sermon which he directs to the longshoremen:

"... Some people think the Crucifixion only took place on Calvary. They better wise up... Dropping a sling on "K.O." Dugan because he was ready to spill his guts tomorrow—that's a crucifixion. And every time the mob puts the crusher on a good man—tries to stop him from doing his duty as a citizen—it's a crucifixion. And anybody who sits around and lets it happen—keeps silent about something he knows has happened—shares the guilt of it just as much as the Roman soldier who pierced the flesh of Our Lord to see if He was dead. . . . Boys, this is my church! And if you don't think Christ is down here on the waterfront, you've got another guess coming! Every morning when the hiring boss blows his whistle, Jesus stands alongside you in the shape-up. He sees why some of you get picked and some of you get passed over. He sees the family men worrying about getting the rent and getting food in the house for the wife and the kids. He sees you selling your souls to the mob for a day's pay . . .

"And what does Christ think of the easy-money boys who do none of the work and take all the gravy? And how does he feel about the fellows who wear hundred-and-fifty dollar suits and diamond rings, on your union dues and your kickback money? And how does He, who spoke up without fear against every evil, feel about your silence?

"You want to know what's wrong with our waterfront? It's the love of a lousy buck. It's making the love of the lousy buck—the cushy job—more important than the love of man! It's forgettin' that every fellow down here is your brother in Christ! But remember, Christ is always with you—Christ is in the shape up. He's in the hatch . . . He's kneeling right here beside Dugan. And He's saying with all of you, if you do it to the

least of mine, you do it to me! And what they did
to Joey, and what they did to Dugan, they are
doing to you. And you. You. ALL OF YOU. And
only you, only you with God's help, have the
power to knock 'em off for good."[2]

It's a Wonderful Life is one of the best loved American
classics. It tells the story of George Bailey (James Stewart)
who throughout his life longs for excitement and adventure through travel away from the small town of Bedford
Falls. Married with five children George feels trapped in
his work at the Savings and Loan and believes he could
find fulfillment in more exotic locales. When he is about to
be falsely accused of financial fraud, George seriously
contemplates suicide. An angel Clarence (Henry Travers)
is sent to help him and the angel succeeds by showing
George that he has had a wonderful life.

The film is both very humorous and deeply touching.
What should not be missed is the very important religious
dimension. The film opens with shots of different homes
in Bedford Falls. We hear voices praying for George
Bailey. Just before George despairs and is going to commit
suicide he prays to God for help. Late in the film, after he
realizes how wonderful his life has been, he prays to God
to release him from the suspended existence he has had
while looking back on his entire life with Clarence as his
guide. He prays "I want to live again. I want to live again.
Please, God, let me live again." When George is reunited
with his family, he and all his friends end the film by
singing the hymn "Hark the Herald Angels Sing" and
then "Auld Lang Syne." The hymn tells of God's love for
us, the song celebrates the love of neighbor. Even though

It's a Wonderful Life is a comedy, it is profoundly religious and reveals Frank Capra's Christian vision. Capra once wrote:

"Comedy is fulfillment, accomplishment, overcoming. It is victory over odds, a triumph of good over evil . . .

"Comedy is good news... The Gospels are comedies; a triumph of spirit over matter. The Resurrection is the happiest of all endings: man's triumph over death. The Mass is celebration of that event. Priests and parishioners celebrate a Mass. It is a divine comedy." [3]

After World War II, Capra made a statement about the kind of films he wanted to make in the future. In his statement he said:

". . . my films must let every man, woman and child know that God loves them and that I love them, and that peace and salvation will become a reality only when they all learn to love each other." [4]

Certainly Capra achieved that goal with *It's a Wonderful Life* but even before he made the statement he had made some wonderful films. Among my favorite films are at least four that were directed by Frank Capra: *It's a Wonderful Life, Mr. Smith Goes to Washington, Meet John Doe* and *Mr. Deeds Goes to Town*. James Stewart starred in *Mr. Smith* and *It's a Wonderful Life,* Gary Cooper starred in *Mr. Deeds* and *Meet John Doe*. In all four films the main character seems clearly to be a "Christ figure," battling evil and succeeding by means of his own suffering. When he was directing the films how conscious Capra was that he was making his heroes "Christ figures" is anybody's guess.

Many realities can influence our consciousness and conscience. There is much in the contemporary world that can drag us down. Certainly film can have a very negative influence on us. A steady diet of violent and sexually exploitative films has to have some impact on people. Some very talented artists are involved in the making of movies, and what they produce can change the way people view themselves, their neighbors and God. Just as a steady diet of violent and sexually exploitative films can have a negative influence on people, excellent films can have a positive influence. Film can be one of the great contemporary arts and can touch people deeply. Great films can help us reflect on what is important in human living. A good religious film can deepen our understanding of ourselves, of our neighbors and of God.

At the end of the year 2000 there was an international congress held in Rome whose theme was "John Paul and the Cinema: A Journey of Faith and Culture, Art and Communication." During the meeting there was a debate between two film directors about the possibility of having a genuinely Catholic cinema. I wish I could have been there. The topic fascinates me and I think it is very important. It is something about which Catholics should think seriously. In introducing the debate, someone referred to the pope as an attentive student of the cinema, a student who looks for the spark of the divine in human experience and profoundly loves artists. I love that expression "spark of the divine." The pope takes cinema seriously and so should we.

I was told that in the debate one director said that she hoped that no one would produce Catholic cinema and that she did not even like the label; the other director disagreed and pointed out that a Catholic artist runs into many closed doors and is looked upon with skepticism by colleagues. He insisted that Catholic artists have something to present to the world and they must present it even if it causes them to be isolated.

I wish I had the opportunity to dialogue with each director in order to be certain what each meant. My suspicion is that I would find truth in each of their views. The key point in the discussion is what is meant by the term "Catholic cinema." My guess is that what one director wanted was a cinema that was not overtly religious and certainly not denominational but a cinema which focuses honestly on the human mystery. I am greatly in favor of films which intelligently deal explicitly with Catholic faith. I think of Robert Bresson's *The Diary of a Country Priest*, *The Mission*, *The Keys of the Kingdom*, *The Green Years*. However films that deal explicitly with Catholic faith are rare and in trying to make them the artist must be careful not to make a film that is more catechetical than artistic. I do believe that there is an attitude of suspicion that many have toward artists who are religious and who allow their religious faith to influence their art. There seem to be critics who are tolerant and even sympathetic to every message except a religious message.

Andrew Greeley co-authored a fascinating book, *God in the Movies*, which sees religious themes in all sorts of films which ordinarily would not be categorized as religious films. In the preface to the book Roger Ebert, the well known film critic, writes:

> "Maybe we are embarrassed to discuss religion and the movies at the same time. Perhaps when we have spiritual experiences we translate them into mundane terms as quickly as we can. I know that I have been shaken to the depth of my existence by a few movies (*Do the Right Thing, Cries and Whispers, Ikiru* for example), and I also know that even broadly popular films such as *Ghost, Field of Dreams,* and *The Sixth Sense* got people worked up. The studios can never understand it when a film like *The Sixth Sense,* which is mostly downbeat, contemplative, and deliberately confusing, attracts enormous audiences and repeat business. It is because it gives people something to talk about and think about, and they appreciate it. One of the values of this book is that it considers the ways in which those films may have touched many of the members of their audiences—whether they were prepared to admit it or not." [5]

I agree completely with Ebert. Right now it seems the value of movies is not appreciated, not even by those who make them. What a strange situation! Even their creators don't realize how powerful films can be.

In the last three or four years I have given two retreats in which film played a key role. When the idea was first proposed to me that I should give a retreat with film as the background I was not sure I liked the idea but the more I thought about it the more appealing it became to me. Planning the retreat I found that my ideas went in two directions. I started to think about what films might be used and at the same time I thought about what mysteries of faith might be reflected on and explored. Very soon, at least in my mind, the two directions became one and both films and topics seemed to coalesce. The retreat forced me to think about the difference between art and religion, between an intense aesthetic experience and a religious, mystical experience.

God Speaks through Movies

Films do not have to deal explicitly with religious subjects to have a religious dimension to them. The experience of great art, while it may not always provide a direct religious experience, is a spiritual experience and may not only increase the viewer's appreciation of art but also the viewer's appreciation of life. The great film might lead the viewer to reflection on his or her own life. I think a great film can indirectly foster religious life by brilliantly depicting some aspect of the human mystery.

During the retreats I wanted to have films that can lead directly to religious reflection on the meaning of God and our relationship to God. This not only required a careful selection of films but also required that an atmosphere be created so that films would be viewed not just for entertainment or even only for artistic appreciation. Rather I wanted our approach to the films to be "How is God speaking to me through this movie?" Just as we can miss God's self-disclosure through other realities, we can miss it in films. My concern during the retreats was to create an atmosphere so that God could be heard in the films shown. I wanted to encourage the retreatants to view the films prayerfully.

The two retreats, one for priests and one for lay people, were based on the concept of story. What I was hoping would happen on the retreats was that all of us would see more clearly and appreciate more deeply the presence of the Holy Spirit in our lives. I tried to stress that each of our stories is more marvelous than any one of us could appreciate. My hope in using the films was that they would become sacramental for us during the retreat. If we remind ourselves that God is everywhere, waiting for us to respond to His self-gift to us, then it is obvious that anything can be a channel of God's grace for us. Whatever calls our attention to the presence of God in our lives can serve a sacramental function for us. I believe that great stories can be channels of God's grace. They can call our attention to the presence of the Holy Spirit and so can help us to grow closer to God. The films I chose are great stories and so I hoped that they would affect the retreatants "sacramentally."

Three of the films that I chose to illuminate the meaning of priesthood on the retreat for priests were *Dead Man Walking*, *The Keys of the Kingdom*, and *Cry, the Beloved Country*. Because *Dead Man Walking* has as its main character not a priest, but Sister Helen Prejean, the Catholic sister who works with prisoners on death row, it might seem strange that I chose it as a film that can illuminate the meaning of priesthood. Throughout this tremendous film, Sister Helen tries to get a convicted killer who is on death row to take responsibility for the evil he has done. This is precisely what a priest should do. So, even though the character was not a priest, the film had some marvelous insights into the meaning of priesthood.

Based on A.J. Cronin's novel, *The Keys of the Kingdom* contains a terrific performance by Gregory Peck. Some viewers might find the film excessively sentimental, but I think it is exceptionally good. The novel and the film tell the story of a Scottish diocesan priest who spends most of his priestly ministry in China. The notion that a priest is called to serve others comes through beautifully in the film. Also the film successfully depicts some beautiful friendships that the priest has because of his priesthood.

I think that *Cry, the Beloved Country* is one of the greatest religious films ever made. The film is based on Alan Paton's novel and it tells the story of an Anglican priest who is like a contemporary Job. His faith in God is severely tested and yet he remains a man of great faith. That a film of this caliber ran for only a week or so in Manhattan when it opened a few years ago is a terrible commentary on the present situation of film in this country. *Cry, the Beloved Country* may be the best film ever made about suffering and trusting in God's love. Those who created the film, including actors James Earl Jones and Charles Dutton, ought to be very proud of their accomplishment. They created a religious masterpiece.

I know of no problem that so regularly either moves people closer to God or away from God as the problem of suffering. When people experience suffering, either their own or the suffering of loved ones, they often interpret it as a sign of their vulnerability, finitude and limitation. This sign leads them to place themselves in God's hands. The experience of suffering for most of us seems to be a call to a deeper faith and hope. People who experience suffering as a sign of their dependence on God will often say that what looked like disaster turned out to be a blessing because it led them to a closer relationship with God. My mother was fond of saying "Everything happens for the best." Though I would not articulate the insight exactly the same as my mother articulated it, I do think the basic insight she had was the same as St. Paul's: "for those who love God all things work together unto good." That God can draw good out of everything should be the source of great consolation and comfort for us. Sometimes we can see God drawing good out of evil and at other times we just have to believe and trust.

There are people whose experience of suffering seems to move them away from God. I could not count the number of people I have met who claimed that they have given up the practice of their faith because of some suffering or tragedy that has befallen them or their loved ones. We can all recall people whose experience of suffering has been interpreted by them as either a sign that God does not exist or that God has abandoned them.

Unfortunately, many people who have given up their faith because of suffering, seem to have a strange view of God. They seem to think that if you pray to God and try to live a good life, then you will be blessed in this life and no crosses will enter your life. It's as though they have a deal with God: "I will do this for You but that means that You must bless me and my loved ones in this life so that no suffering befalls either me or them." I wonder how that view of God arose. It seems to be so far from the Christian view of God. What about the suffering of Jesus? Could any human being have been better than Jesus and yet He suffered terribly? Unfortunately, some believers tend to think that because of His divinity Jesus did not really suffer but only appeared to be suffering, but Christian faith is that the Son of God *really* suffered and *really* died. Any meaning that a Christian can derive from suffering has to be linked to the suffering and death of Jesus.

What makes *Cry, the Beloved Country* such a great religious film is that it does not flinch in dealing with the Christian view of suffering. Everything that the Anglican priest holds dear seems to be taken away from him and yet, in the midst of this terrible suffering, he remains a man of faith.

Another marvelous religious film is *Places in the Heart.* It tells the story of a young widowed mother, played beautifully by Sally Field, who has to struggle to keep her land and bring up her two children. At the beginning of the film her husband, the sheriff of the small town in Mississippi where he and his family lived, is accidentally shot by a young drunken black man. The youth is tied to a truck and dragged through the town and then his body is hung from a tree. His funeral and the funeral of the dead sheriff take place in the same town but in different cemeteries, one for black people and one for white people. This violent heart-breaking opening sets the scene for a drama that deeply explores human relationships and love. The film ends with a communion service. The minister reads from St. Paul about Jesus giving his body and blood to his disciples and then passes the communion wafers and the wine to the congregants. As those in the church receive communion the camera slowly pans the faces of the congregants. The last two people we see sharing communion are the sheriff and the young black who killed him. This surrealistic depiction of Christians receiving communion may be the greatest eucharistic scene in any American film.

Woody Allen: Asking Religious Questions

I really like Woody Allen's films. No author/director working in the American film industry can come close to Allen in talent and insight. More than any other contemporary American artist, Allen has created a large number of outstanding films. I have followed his career closely and one of the most impressive aspects is that Allen the artist seems to be getting better and better. That does not necessarily mean that each new film he turns out is better than the previous ones but there does seem to be perceptible growth in his career over the years.

The screen persona who has appeared in almost all of Allen's films and who is usually played by Allen himself is a loser who cannot believe in God and cannot enter into a successful love relationship with a woman. Woody seems to link together the absence of a loving God with the failure of human beings to communicate lovingly with one another. The so-called silence of God casts a shadow over all attempts at love commitments. Allen's screen persona is preoccupied with death and also often preoccupied with art. Once again I can understand someone not liking Allen's work, which is a matter of taste, or even his lifestyle. But I would disagree with anyone who thinks that he is not an exceptionally gifted filmmaker.

Over the years different Allen films have appealed to me for different reasons. I know some of his fans like his earlier films, which seem less serious. Though all of Allen's films, with the exception of *Interiors* (1978), have some humor in them, as his career has progressed Allen has been devoting more screen time to serious issues. I think that the more serious films raise the most important questions about life and I think that in putting this on film Allen is unique among directors of contemporary comedies and indeed unique among contemporary American directors.

For a time each Woody Allen film seemed to top his last one. His talent seemed to be expanding. Some of the films that I found especially interesting are *Annie Hall* (1977), *Stardust Memories* (1980), *Broadway Danny Rose* (1984), *The Purple Rose of Cairo* (1985), *Crimes and Misdemeanors* (1989), *Alice* (1991) and *Celebrity* (1999).

In *Annie Hall* Allen explores the difficulty of entering into a permanent love relationship in the contemporary world. At the end of the film, Alvy Singer (Woody Allen) and the woman he loves, Annie, have broken up. He wonders about the possibility of a permanent interpersonal relationship and why people keep trying to relate in love. He says it reminds him of a joke. A woman confesses to a friend that her brother has a psychological problem—he thinks he is a chicken. Her friend asks "Why don't you tell him he is not a chicken?" The woman replies "We need the eggs!" People have to try to relate.

Stardust Memories is an extremely clever take-off on Federico Fellini's masterpiece *8½*. I have often thought that sometime it would be fun to study the two films together. Allen, I believe, even copies Fellini's camera setups and angles. In the film, Sandy Bates (Woody Allen) who is a film director, is wondering what his next film project should be. At one point he has a vision of a muse and he asks the muse what he should do with his life, whether he should spend his time working with the poor. The muse responds "Tell better jokes."

Broadway Danny Rose is about a talent agent who is exceptionally kind and considerate to all his clients, but is betrayed by one of them. Danny Rose's attitude toward his clients is summed up in his statement, "Acceptance, forgiveness, love." Allen borrows from the great Japanese director Akira Kurosowa's *Rashomon* (1950), and begins his film with a group of stand-up comics reminiscing about Danny Rose and giving different perspectives on his life.

The Purple Rose of Cairo is a very clever and amusing film about how films so affect us that it is difficult for some moviegoers to tell what is real and what is fantasy.

My favorite Allen film is *Crimes and Misdemeanors* (1989). In the film a successful ophthalmologist, Dr. Judah Rosenthal (Martin Landau), in order to conceal an extramarital affair from his wife, arranges for the murder of his mistress. Landau, in a great performance, conveys the confused conscience of Dr. Rosenthal. Brought up in a religious home, Dr. Rosenthal knows that his extra-marital affair is immoral and he knows that having his mistress murdered is seriously sinful but he chooses what is expedient. Rather than confess his sins to his wife, he chooses to eliminate his girlfriend. The doctor seems to live happily ever after with his wife. The film raises serious moral and religious questions. If there is a God then why would a murderer be able to live happily in this world; and if there is no God, how can we decide what is and what is not immoral? *Crimes and Misdemeanors* is a brilliant film and deeply religious.

Alice has probably the most upbeat ending of any Woody Allen film. Alice is a wealthy Upper East Side lady who leads a rather pampered existence. Her background is Catholic, but her faith does not seem to have much effect on her life. When she discovers that her husband has been unfaithful, she goes to India for a time to work with Mother Teresa and then commits herself to working with poor children in New York. One of her friends, in commenting on Alice's dramatic change, says "It's that Catholic thing." I can still recall the day that I saw *Alice*. Later that day, I felt a kind of glow. That's how uplifting I found the film. The experience of it colored the rest of my day. I thought that it was just marvelous that Woody Allen had equated "that Catholic thing" with working with Mother Teresa and with helping the poor.

What I like best about *Celebrity* is its message. Once again, Allen gives us a character who cannot relate and who seems terribly mixed up. The character played by Kenneth Branagh seems to be the contemporary man who has been in every Allen film. He is unsuccessful in his relationships and can make no sense of life. The message of the movie is "Help!"

It might seem that I am pushing things when I claim that Allen's films are religious but I do think that they are. Clearly they are very moral films, but I see them as both moral and religious, because Allen, in each film, is exploring how human beings can be fulfilled and whether there is any point to human living. So far Allen, with the exception of *Alice,* has not depicted a solution to the human condition that I find correct. However, the fact that he continues to make films that raise important philosophical and religious questions is a tremendous gift to those who take films seriously.

Five Films Too Fine to Be Forgotten

During this time in the history of films when many creators of film seem only interested in making the blockbuster, the movie mega-hit that will gross a huge fortune at the box office, I have been especially aware of a handful of films that I have seen in the last ten years that are exceptionally good but did not reach large audiences in theaters. It saddens me that, while people flock to see relatively mindless blockbusters, these films went largely unseen. I will use five films to illustrate that there are marvelous films made that never got the audience they deserve. The five films I have chosen are two about the Holocaust, *The Revolt of Job* and *Shoah,* and *The Color of Paradise, Wide Awake* and *The Big Kahuna.*

The Revolt of Job is the type of film that can restore someone's faith in the power of art to touch us deeply, to instruct us, to inspire and even to sanctify us. The plot of the film centers around Job and his wife Roza, an elderly farming couple who live in a small village in East Hungary. The year is 1943. The couple has tried time and again to have a healthy offspring. All of their seven children have died; and, because of their age, time is running out for them. Job decides to break the law and adopt a Christian child and raise him for God. The boy, who is seven years of age, is extremely unruly; but eventually, through love, Job and Roza tame him. As the Holocaust is spreading to the small farming village, Job, who knows that he and his wife will be arrested, is determined that his son will not be taken. I won't reveal the ending of the film except to say that it is deeply religious.

Shoah, Claude Lanzmann's documentary on the Holocaust, is outstanding. The film is nine and a half hours long. Certainly the length of the film contributed to its power. What Lanzmann does is allow survivors of the Holocaust to speak about their experiences. Lanzmann either photographs a survivor in close-up or, as a survivor's voice is heard, the camera focuses on some area about which the survivor is speaking. For example, the camera might show the site of a concentration camp or the train tracks used by the trains which carried thousands of Jews to their extermination. The structure of the film is simple but its power is almost overwhelming.

There is one scene that I initially found shocking but ultimately found heartbreaking. The scene shows a Jewish barber working in his barbershop. He is cutting the hair of a man, and several other male customers seem to be waiting for haircuts. The barber is explaining how during the war he cut the hair of women just before they were gassed to death. The women's hair had to be cut before they were murdered because the Nazis sold the hair which could be used for wigs. The barber told how he was enlisted and told to find several other barbers to work with him. He told how the women, stark naked, were brought into a room and how he and other male barbers cut their hair. The women thought that they were going to showers. Moments later the women would be dead. In a very matter of fact manner the barber talks about the style of haircut he gave and about how quickly the hair could be cut and about how many women he could serve in an hour. I was stunned as I watched him speak. How could he speak of this experience as though he was telling about some job he once had in a beauty parlor?

After about ten minutes of screen time the barber starts to mention an experience he had when two women he knew personally were led in to have their hair cut. Suddenly he stops speaking. His manner changes dramatically. He begins to cry. He cannot speak. He asks Lanzmann to turn off the camera saying that he cannot continue. He holds a towel up to his face. Lanzmann, off camera, says that he knows how difficult this must be for the barber but he begs him to continue. The barber says that he cannot continue and tries to walk off camera. He stands there crying, wiping his face with the towel. Eventually he is able to compose himself enough to continue to tell his tale of horror.

I realized that the original apparent coolness and detachment of the barber was the only way that he could even speak about the terrible experience he had in relation to the extermination of the women. As his memory went back to those terrible days, he had to try to control himself and assume an emotional distance from the horrible events he had experienced.

Philosophically the film revealed the beauty of human persons. By contrasting the Jewish people, who endured so much, with the Nazis, who were so cruel, Lanzmann's film conveyed a profound ethical message. Freedom is one of God's greatest gifts to us, but freedom can be misused. Freedom can lead to love and commitment but freedom also led to the Holocaust. Shoah is a film which calls us to remember but also calls us to examine how we treat people.

Viewing the Iranian film *The Color of Paradise* is like experiencing a lovely poem or even receiving the powerful effect of reading a spiritual classic. The plot revolves around an eight-year-old blind boy, Mohammad, whose widowed father wants to be rid of him so he can be more free. The boy's grandmother loves the boy very much and is opposed to the father's plan to give his son off to a blind carpenter under the pretense that the lad will learn a trade.

Early in the film some of the themes are suggested. The school for the blind that the boy attends is closing for the summer. The boy's father is late in coming to pick him up; and when he finally arrives, he pleads with school authorities to take the boy for the summer, claiming that he cannot take care of him. While waiting for his father, the boy explores some of the area outside the school. Hearing the chirping of a small bird, the boy with his hands feels through piles of leaves until he discovers the baby bird who has fallen from a nest. Using his extraordinary sense of hearing and touch, the boy finds the tree from which the bird has fallen and in which the bird's parent is chirping, climbs it and restores the baby to the nest. This beautiful scene reveals both Mohammad's intelligence and his goodness. Unfortunately the boy's father is not as concerned about his son as the boy is about the bird.

Throughout the film there are breathtaking shots of nature. The sensitivity of the blind boy to nature is exceptional. In fact, the young actor, Mohsen Ramezani, is amazing in conveying the blind boy's exceptional intelligence and emotional depth. When he realizes that he is with the carpenter because his father does not want him, Mohammad breaks down in tears. He explains to the carpenter that he is crying because no one wants him due to his blindness. Being consoled by the blind carpenter, the young boy says that one of his teachers in school told him that when he reaches out to touch things, he is really reaching out to touch God and that eventually he will reach God. This gives a new meaning to the many shots of Mohammad's hands reaching out. The boy's hand at the end of the film suggests a profoundly religious meaning and works wonderfully to sum up what is most important in this excellent film.

Before his exceptionally successful *A Sixth Sense*, M. Nigh Shyamalan wrote and directed the film *Wide Awake* that opened and closed quickly. *Wide Awake* is a marvelous movie, a lovely, simple film that explores crucial philosophical and religious questions. With gentle humor and marvelous insights into the human mystery, the film depicts the fifth grade Catholic school experience of Joshua Beal (Joseph Cross) as he tries to find the answers to life's most difficult questions.

Months prior to Joshua starting fifth grade, his grandfather (Robert Loggia) died. Missing the beautiful loving presence of his grandfather, Joshua has fallen into a depression. The film opens with a scene of Joshua being unable to wake up and get out of bed in the morning because of his deep depression. The death of his grandfather has so changed Joshua's experience of the world that nothing seems to matter to him. Grandpa Beal, while suffering with his terminal illness, had told Joshua not to worry about him because "God will take care of me." Joshua wonders if God is taking care of his deceased loved one, indeed Joshua wonders if God exists.

The film depicts Joshua's determined efforts to find some answers. He is on a search that we rarely see in feature films. I confess that if author/producer/director Shyamalan had asked me what possibility he had of getting his film made, I would have said zero to none. Thank heaven that Shyamalan had the courage and confidence to create this movie, which was his first feature film. Admitting that he tapped his own childhood experience in writing *Wide Awake*, Shyamalan made the following comments about his story:

> "I was looking for an inspirational story. For a long time, I had the idea of a kid coming to terms with the aftermath of his grandfather's death— remembering his grandfather saying to him, 'You know, I'll be all right because God will take care of me.' And suddenly this kid needs to know for sure, is it true? Is Grandpa all right? What I loved about it is that this is the biggest question you can ask. But because he's a kid, Joshua is determined to find out the exact answer for himself no matter what it takes. He really believes that, if he tries hard enough, he can just go out and find that answer."[6]

Eventually Joshua does find his answer, but he is helped along the way by several people. One is Sister Terry (Rosie O'Donnell). Others are his friends, his sister, his parents and a boy he tries to help. How Joshua finds his answers is particularly striking. In order to solve his interior problems, he has to come out of himself and become interested in other human beings. That solution is not only psychologically and philosophically right but also theologically correct. What is amazing is that while dealing with profound issues, Shyamalan succeeds in keeping his film simple. The film can be viewed on several levels and so it is in the best sense of the term a "family picture." Anyone who has experienced the loss of a loved one can sympathize with Joshua as he tries to make sense of his experience. *Wide Awake* is a film that members of the family could discuss after seeing it. The film raises the right questions and I think gives some beautiful answers.

Shyamalan's story, which takes place in the course of the school year, is divided into three sections which Shyamalan entitles "September: the question;" "December: the signs;" and "May: the answers." Throughout the film Shyamalan mixes humor with important insights into love, suffering and the mystery of God's presence in our lives. I found especially touching the relationship between Joshua and the grandfather. Actor Robert Loggia does a fine job of conveying the man's enormous love for his grandson and his concern that the boy learns the right values. With simplicity and directness *Wide Awake* depicts the grandfather's Catholic faith beautifully. By the end of the film Joshua can get out of bed in the morning with some ease. The title of the film refers to Joshua's coming out of his depression. It also refers to "seeing things the way they really are," which is another way of saying "seeing reality through the eyes of religious faith."

An apostolate that I am involved in at St. John's University is an annual film festival conducted by the Vincentian Center for Church and Society. The festival always has a theme related to society and justice. I choose the films and I am delighted to be involved with the festival because I see it as an opportunity to educate students at St. John's concerning the value and importance of film. The year that the theme of the festival was "Human Work" I was determined to have the film *The Big Kahuna* as part of the festival.

When *The Big Kahuna* was first released I brought two of my friends to see it and we doubled the attendance in the theater! The film was not a huge commercial success! But it is a great film, and I was determined that I would do what I could to have others, especially students at St. John's, see it. In festivals that I am involved with, I try to avoid films that have four-letter words in them because I have come to believe that some screenwriters, instead of writing intelligent dialogue, pepper their scripts with profanities. This time I made an exception because I think *The Big Kahuna* is an exceptionally good film and should be seen by adults who are interested in dramas that deal with serious questions. The audience's reaction to the film at the festival and especially the comments from students told me that I had made the right judgment.

The plot centers around three salesmen attending a business convention for their firm. One (Danny De Vito) has recently been divorced and is questioning the meaning of his life. Another (Kevin Spacey) seems to be a complete skeptic. The third (Peter Facinelli) is a young, recently married, born-again Christian. Most of the film takes place in their motel room as they discuss how to make a big deal at the convention. The real action of the movie is their arguing about what is really important in their lives.

I suppose what pleased me first on the evening we screened *The Big Kahuna* was the size of the student turnout. For four or five years I had been trying to interest students in film classics without great success. Unfortunately two questions that some students ask about film are "How old is this film?" and "Is it in color?" Student interest in film has waned dramatically since the 1960s. Forty years ago many college students had a strong interest in art films and at that time interest in serious films was not limited to college students. Many people in the '60s came to the realization that film was the art form of the 20th century, including within itself all the other arts.

One reason that I have been encouraging students in my philosophy classes at St. John's to become interested in serious film is that film can raise all sorts of important philosophical questions. A danger today is that so much of contemporary cinema is either so mindless or shallow that a constant diet of such fare can greatly influence a person's taste and shrink a viewer's horizons. What pleased me even more than the number of students at *The Big Kahuna* was their reaction. After each film at a festival there is a question and answer period. The one following *The Big Kahuna* was exceptionally good. At one point a student stood up and said something like "The difference between this movie and the junk you usually see in theaters is that this film makes you think." At that moment I knew that the festival was working, that the film had really touched the audience. Other students made similar comments. Education can take place in all sorts of settings. The classroom can be one. A theater can be another. Some people, who do not have the advantage of studying philosophy formally, can be exposed to philosophical questions through great films. Those who have both the opportunity to study philosophy and to see great cinema are doubly blessed. There is a scene in *The Big Kahuna* when Danny De Vito and Kevin Spacey discuss God and whether they believe in God. The scene is marvelous. I cannot recall any recent American film that has a scene like it. During that scene a great silence fell over the audience. It was one of several moments during the screening of *The Big Kahuna* when I knew that I had chosen the right film.

Questions for Reflection

1. How could a film that presents a false view of human nature indirectly foster religious experience? Can you think of an example?
2. Did you see *On the Waterfront?* Do you agree with Father Lauder's analysis of it? Did you see *It's A Wonderful Life?* Do you agree with Father Lauder's comments on it? Do you think these films can be channels of God's Revelation?
3. Can you explain how the title characters in *Mr. Deeds Goes to Town, Mr. Smith Goes to Washington* and *Meet John Doe* are Christ figures?

4. Why might the use of film on a retreat be a good idea?
5. Can you suggest how the films *Dead Man Walking, The Keys of the Kingdom* and *Cry, the Beloved Country* might mediate God's Revelation to us?
6. Can you think of any Woody Allen film which is religious? If so, why do you think it can be considered religious?
7. Can you comment on any of the five "forgotten films" that Father Lauder says should not be forgotten?

---

[1] John Paul II, *Letter to Artists, op. cit.*, p. 4.

[2] *On the Waterfront*, 1954.

[3] *The Name Above the Title* (New York: The Macmillan Company, 1971), p. 453.

[4] Ibid., p. 375.

[5] Roger Ebert's preface to Andrew Greeley's *God in the Movies* (New Jersey: Transaction Publishers, New Brunswick, 2000), p. IX.

[6] MIRAMAX Production Notes, p. 10 (Film released in 1997).

3

The Magic of Theater

My vocation as a priest-philosopher means that for many of my conscious hours I am preoccupied with mystery. Every person's life is surrounded by mystery, but, because of my vocation, I am called to celebrate mystery and to reflect on mystery. As a priest, I celebrate the mystery of God's love in liturgy and in homilies I preach the Word who is the Message and Mystery of God; as philosopher, I probe the mystery of the human person and the meaning of the Divine.

These preoccupations have spilled over into my interest in theater. No piece of drama thrills me more than drama about the mystery of a human person's relationship with God. If I discover that the creators of a play have a special interest in communicating what is most profound and most true about human existence, which for me has to be religious meaning, then my interest has been aroused. A serious danger when someone wants to deal seriously with some religious subject is that the work of art will become merely a piece of propaganda, that while the message might be marvelous, the work of art is poor, nothing more than a slightly concealed sermon. A religious work of art that is a poor work of art may be less revealing of God than a great work of art that ostensibly is not religious art.

A few years ago I attended a memorial service for a person famous in the Broadway theater. It was very beautiful and moving. Actors, a playwright, producers and others spoke glowingly of the deceased and there was not one false note. However, two things struck me about the experience. I was surprised that throughout the service there was not one mention of religion or God. Not one! I thought that strange in a memorial service. The other is that those connected with the theater seemed to have substituted art for religion in their own lives. Of course, there is no way that I could know that for sure but that was the strong impression I received. Language that was being used during the memorial speeches reminded me of the kind of language that you hear in a church but these words were being uttered in a theater and no references were being made to God or religion.

After the memorial when I mentioned to friends, who know many artists, my impression about the substitution of art for religion, without a second's hesitation they agreed with me. One question that is on my mind is why traditional religion seems to have so little meaning or appeal to so many serious artists? Is it a matter of upbringing? Is it a matter of poor religious education or even no religious education at all? Is it that the secular age in which we live just has made it impossible for many intellectuals to take religion seriously?

Artistic and Religious Experience

My other questions are about what there is in art and the experience of art that allows so many to substitute it for religion. Is it the spiritual dimension of art? Does some art provide a vision of life that easily substitutes for a religious vision? Is an intense artistic or aesthetic experience the same as a religious experience? Is there a mystical dimension to art? Is every artistic experience also a mystical experience? God is everywhere and God can be encountered anywhere. Yet, I do not think that what I ordinarily call an artistic experience or an aesthetic experience is the same as a religious experience or a prayer experience. I think of an artistic experience or an aesthetic experience, for example a profound thought while viewing a play or a film, as an intense experience of beauty. Of course, the experience is beautiful because ultimately God, Unlimited Beauty, is present in it just as sunsets and mountains are beautiful because God is present in them. But just as God is not the sunsets or the mountains but is present in them, so too God is not the play or film but is the ultimate source of their beauty.

In a religious or prayer experience, we encounter God directly not indirectly. We open ourselves to God, so to speak, face to face. So if the artistic experience or aesthetic experience stays on the artistic or aesthetic level, it is an experience of beauty but not a religious experience. However, can artistic or aesthetic experiences move us toward a religious experience? I think they can. In his letter to artists Pope John Paul wrote:

> "Even beyond its typically religious expressions, true art has a close affinity with the world

of faith, so that, even in situations where culture and the Church are far apart, art remains a kind of bridge to religious experience. In so far as it seeks the beautiful, fruit of an imagination which rises above the everyday, art is by its nature a kind of appeal to the mystery. Even when they explore the darkest depths of the soul or the most unsettling aspects of evil, artists give voice in a way to the universal desire for redemption." [2]

Just as an experience of a sunset or a mountain, which is initially just an experience of nature, might move us to prayer, so too an experience of a great play might move us toward God. What starts out as an artistic experience might become a religious experience or an experience of prayer.

The Depth of Human Experience

I can recall an exceptionally interesting class from a college English course I took fifty years ago. The teacher was trying to illustrate what a "moment of theater" was. He probably gave a few examples, but the one that has stayed with me all these years was from the production of *The Death of a Salesman* starring Lee J. Cobb. The teacher created one scene for us very vividly. What he was describing as a "moment of theater" was some moment of a play that was so vivid and powerful that it stood out both dramatically and also thematically, a moment that illustrated the magic of theater.

The "moment" that he chose from Arthur Miller's classic was the scene in which salesman Willie Loman's two sons invite him out to dinner, ostensibly to celebrate a changing point in their careers. While in the men's room, Willie discovers that there is nothing to celebrate, that like himself, his sons are failures in business. He suspects that his favorite son, Biff, is deliberately a failure in order to punish Willie, whom he caught committing adultery many years previously. Willie goes down on both knees on the floor of the bathroom and pounds the floor. I think to illustrate the "moment" my teacher pounded on the desk. He claimed that Willie's pounding on the floor was a "moment of theater."

I did see the film version of Arthur Miller's play, starring Frederic March, back in 1951. While studying as a seminarian in the summer of 1959 at The Catholic University of America, I saw Myron McCormick star in a production at the University's theater. A few years ago I saw Ralph Waite star in Miller's play at The Sawmill River Playhouse in New Jersey. None of these versions prepared me for the experience of seeing Brian Dennehy play Willie Loman in the Broadway production in 1999. I wonder what "moments of theater" my professor would have found in that exceptional production! Seeing Dennehy play Loman is one of the five or six greatest experiences I have had in the theater. "Brilliant" is one of the words that comes to mind to describe both Dennehy's performance and the production of this American classic.

What amazes me is how a group of artists can take a play that has been done thousands of times and breathe new life into it, uncover new meanings in it and present it in such a way that someone attending feels that he or she is seeing the play for the first time or at least seeing it in a new way. That was certainly my experience of the 1999 production. All sorts of meanings that I had either never attended to or that were not highlighted in previous productions that I had seen became evident to me. Several times while watching the play I had the feeling of making a new discovery.

Everyone in this production of *The Death of a Salesman* turned in fine performances, but Dennehy was something special. From now on any actor who tries to perform Willie Loman will be measured against Dennehy's performance. The production stressed Willie's gradually losing touch with reality. Even the sets suggest that we have somehow entered Willie's mind in which the present and past, the real and the imagined, can no longer be distinguished. Dennehy frequently put the fingers of his right hand up to his temple and almost seemed to be trying to massage clarity into his mind. That gesture of his facial expressions, especially when he thought he had discovered a new way for him or his sons to be successful in business, conveyed a man's entire life. Great theater is magical and can shed light on the human mystery for us. The 1999 production of *The Death of a Salesman* did that.

A genuine moment of theater occurred in this production after Willie gives some additional advice to Biff about how to relate to the interviewer. He tells Biff that if some papers should fall from the interviewer's desk, Biff should not pick them up but rather remain formal and distant. Later while Willie is trying to get a favor from the head of his company, some papers fall from the desk and Willie stoops over and picks them up. That gesture of stooping and picking up the papers sums up both the failure and confusion of Willie Loman. At the performance I attended, some members of the audience groaned as Willie stooped down.

Through his eyes and facial expressions, Brian Dennehy conveyed that Willie was losing touch with the real world. Willie seems to be looking forward to a better future but when he speaks, we realize that the envisioned future has little to do with reality. His eyes are not seeing as much as imagining or creating. For example, when he is thinking about how his sons would benefit from getting $20,000 from his life insurance policy should he die, Willie fantasizes about how magnificent they will be with that kind of money. Of course, nothing that they have done in business even suggests that they would have any success at all.

As the play peels away the facades that Willie has built around himself, we come to see a character for whom we must feel sorry, for whom we must have compassion. He has been seduced by all the wrong values and has had all the wrong dreams. He has been tricked by the consumer society. A great playwright is able to portray the universal in the singular, to reveal universal truths about human nature through an individual character. Somehow, and I don't know how they do it, great playwrights are able to dramatize the story of one person and to do it in such a way that we are able to see truths about all persons in that character. I do not know anyone exactly like Willie Loman, but somehow in Miller's *The Death of a Salesman*, Willie appears a little bit like all of us. When Willie and Biff embrace near the end of the play and express their love for one another, something universal about family love has been revealed.

When I think of the most important American playwrights I think of Miller, Tennessee Williams and Eugene O'Neill. These three writers have had a tremendous influence on American theater. In plays such as *A Streetcar Named Desire, The Glass Menagerie,* and *The Night of the Iguana* Williams sensitively explores the human mystery. He saw the fragility and vulnerability of persons and he gave us drama that calls to us to reflect on how we treat one another. Among the three, O'Neill is my favorite. I can see some of his plays over and over and each time be deeply moved. His consciousness and his conscience fascinate me. When I think of O'Neill I think of the insight that applies to many "ex-Catholic" artists: you can take the person out of the Church, but you cannot take the Church out of the person.

The Catholicism of Eugene O'Neill

O'Neill was what some people refer to as a "black Irishman." In a book entitled *O'Neill and His Plays: Four Decades of Criticism,* Croswell Bowen has an essay, "The Black Irishman." In the essay Bowen has an excellent description of what those who use the term "black Irishman" mean:

> "The black Irishman . . . is an Irishman who has lost his faith and spends his life searching for the meaning of life, for a philosophy in which he can believe again as fervently as he once believed in the simple answers of the Catholic Catechism. A black Irishman is a brooding solitary man— and often a drinking man, too—with wild words on the tip of his tongue. American letters are

richer for black Irishmen. And of the lot of them, and the list includes F. Scott Fitzgerald, James T. Farrell, and John O'Hara among others, O'Neill is the blackest of all." [3]

Reading Bowen's remarks I am reminded of Dorothy Day's observation about O'Neill. During her early bohemian days in Greenwich Village, Dorothy and Eugene were friends. In the excellent film about Dorothy Day, *Entertaining Angels*, produced by the Paulist priest, Father Elwood Keiser, one of only three feature films produced by the Catholic Church in the United States, the character of O'Neill appears briefly and as I recall makes a typical "black Irishman" remark about the meaning of human existence. Recalling O'Neill, Dorothy described him as absorbed by death and darkness. That description jells with my own experience of O'Neill's plays.

In researching O'Neill's life I discovered that he stopped practicing the Catholic faith when he was about 14 years of age. O'Neill's mother was suffering from drug addiction, and O'Neill prayed fervently for her. That she was not cured apparently was too much of a test for the teenager's faith. He stopped attending Mass and announced that he was never going again. But judging from his plays, I would suggest that he never stopped looking for some answer, some "faith" which would give life some meaning. Many years ago in one of his letters O'Neill wrote the following:

"The playwright today must dig at the roots of the sickness of today as he feels it—the death of God and the failure of science and materialism to give any satisfying new one for the surviving primitive religious instinct to find a meaning for life in and to comfort its fears of death with. It seems to me that anyone trying to do big work nowadays must have this big subject behind the little subjects of his plays or novels, or he is simply scribbling around on the surface of things and has no more real status than a parlor entertainer."[4]

I think that those words can still apply to today's artist. I think that they could be addressed to contemporary playwrights, novelists and perhaps especially to contemporary filmmakers. Contemporary film is tremendously advanced in technology but very low in terms of depth of insight into human life.

I am afraid that many contemporary artists are "simply scribbling around on the surface of things" and are reducing themselves to "parlor entertainers." Great art happens when the artists have the "big subject" behind the little subjects of their plays or novels or films. I don't think we need contemporary art that is "preachy," but we do need artists who can deal with what is most important and deal with it in a way that speaks to our experience.

I am not sure which Eugene O'Neill play is my favorite: *Long Day's Journey into Night* or *A Moon for the Misbegotten.* These two plays reveal both the Catholic consciousness of O'Neill and the desire of a lapsed Catholic for a faith that might replace the Catholic faith he had lost. In a book entitled *Down the Nights and Down the Days: Eugene O'Neill's Catholic Sensibility,* author Edward Shaughnessy quotes a letter that O'Neill at the age of 40 wrote to a friend, Sister Mary Leo Tierney, O.P.:

"There is nothing I would not give to have your faith—the faith in which I was born and brought up (as a good O'Neill should be)—but since I may not know it, since belief is denied to me in spite of the fact that my whole adult spiritual life is that search for a faith which my work expresses in symbols, why then my thwarted search must have its meaning and use, don't you think whatever God may be? Perhaps they also serve who only search in vain! That they search—and not without knowing at times a black despair that believers never know—that is their justification and pride as they stare blindly at the blind sky? The Jesus who said, 'Why hast thou forsaken me?' must surely understand them—and love them a little, I think, and forgive them if no Savior comes today to make the blind to see who may not cure themselves." [5]

When I first read that section of O'Neill's letter I almost cried. I wonder how many artists are in a situation similar to his. Years ago, I read a statement by author Norman Mailer in which he said that he and other artists were looking off into the future for some transcendent meaning, that they could not see it clearly but that they continued to look. The yearning for faith that O'Neill had is almost palpable in the letter and I find enormously touching his honesty and implicit hope that Jesus loves him in spite of his lack of faith. I also find it very moving that he links his own discouragement to Jesus' experience on the cross and that he hopes that there might even be a place in some divine plan for those who search. The sadness that O'Neill had about his inability to believe the Catholic faith colors some of his most important plays.

The film version of *Long Day's Journey into Night* is a truly magnificent piece of work. The acting by Katherine Hepburn, Ralph Richardson, Dean Stockwell and Jason Robards is just about perfect. But O'Neill gave them great characters to portray and Sidney Lumet's direction is exceptionally good. The four members of the Catholic Tyrone family seem unable to help one another and the sins from the past seem inescapable. Mary (Hepburn) was planning to enter a convent until she met James (Richardson) and fell in love with him. Their younger son, Edmund (Stockwell) a stand-in for O'Neill, suffers from consumption. Their elder son, James Jr. (Robards), a drinker and womanizer, resents his father's miserliness which was indirectly the cause of Mary's drug addiction. James Jr. is also envious of Edmund. What O'Neill has given us are four people who love one another but, no matter how they try to heal, continue to hurt one another.

The Catholicism of the father and mother has weakened. The father's faith seems reduced to insisting that Shakespeare was a Catholic, the mother's to recalling her happy days as a young girl with the sisters in Catholic school. Neither seems able to experience anything redemptive. I first read the play when I was a student in the seminary. Someone had a newly published copy. We had a day off from classes, perhaps after exams in January, and I spent much of the day reading the author's strongly autobiographical play. It was a cold rainy day and that fit the mood of the play perfectly.

What never ceases to amaze me is how a new set of artists can give new life and meaning to a classic. That happened with the 1999 Broadway production of *The Death of a Salesman* and it happened again with the 2000 production of O'Neill's *A Moon for the Misbegotten*. Actors Gabriel Byrne, Cherry Jones and Roy Dotrice and director Daniel Sullivan took hold of O'Neill's text and breathed a new life into it. Commenting on the production in *The New York Times*, critic Ben Brantley wrote:

> "Masterpieces, it seems, never stop growing, and the current production emanates both a springtime freshness and an autumnal mellowness. Sullivan and his company have infused the play with a mixture of clear-eyed observation and a warm luminous empathy that melts the performance's solid three hours into a quick-coursing stream. This achievement is the more remarkable when you consider that the script's components examined individually, seem as dense and blunt as the rocks that dominate the landscape of the untillable Connecticut farm on which the play takes place." [6]

A Moon for the Misbegotten is one of the most spiritual plays that I have ever seen, a play about sin, confession and absolution. In a letter probably written in 1925, O'Neill indicated what he was trying to do with his dramas. He wrote that he wanted:

> "to see the transfiguring nobility of tragedy, in as near the Greek sense as one can grasp it, in seemingly the most ignoble, debased lives. And just here is where I am a most confirmed mystic, for

I'm always, always trying to interpret Life in terms of lives, never just in terms of character. I'm always acutely conscious of the force behind—Fate, God, our biological past creating our present, whatever one calls it—Mystery certainly—and of the eternal tragedy of Man in his glorious, self-destructive struggle to make the Force express him instead of being, as an animal is, an infinitesimal incident in its expression." [7]

O'Neill's remarks fit *A Moon for the Misbegotten* beautifully. Though he gave up his Catholic faith while still a teen-ager, O'Neill spent his adult life looking for a vision of reality to replace it. Probably the quotation from the letter is as close to a credo as we have from O'Neill.

In *A Moon for the Misbegotten,* James Tyrone, who is drinking himself to death, has a sin from the past that he can neither forgive himself for or forget. It is a sin he committed against his mother. His guilt drives him to drink, but alcohol provides no real peace. He plans to spend an evening with Josie Hogan, a woman he loves and whom he sees as pure and good. He is hoping that she can be a stand-in for his deceased mother and that if Josie will forgive him, perhaps he will also be forgiven by his mother. Josie is to be his confessor, and he hopes she will absolve him. What Cherry Jones and Gabriel Byrne, especially Byrne, accomplished on the stage during the confession and absolution scene was theatrical magic. Jones is an exceptional actress, and Byrne seemed to be acting with every inch of his body. Or rather he did not seem to be acting at all. He seemed to be experiencing Tyrone's guilt and suffering right in front of us. So brilliant was Byrne that he seemed to be the character, James Tyrone, and I wondered how Byrne could do this every performance. What did it cost him? I don't think there is any confession-absolution scene in any drama that can compare to what happens in *A Moon for the Misbegotten*.

There is one O'Neill play that I have always wanted to see and it may be his most Catholic, though not his greatest play. It is *Days without End*, in which O'Neill splits his main character, John Loving, a Catholic apostate, into two in order to highlight the spiritual struggle going on within the character. "John" is a kind of Faustian character and "Loving" is a kind of Mephistopheles. While "John" is yearning for salvation, "Loving" symbolizes enmity to God. At the end of the play, the apostate returns to the Church. I am not surprised that once O'Neill said that the end of the play was a wish fulfillment on his part.

Director Jose Quintero, who had an enormous influence on the revival of interest in O'Neill, died in February 1999. I knew him slightly but well enough to want to attend the memorial service that was held for him at the Circle in the Square Theater. The memorial service was beautiful and the booklet that was distributed to those who attended the service was a marvelous tribute to this sensitive artist who spent his professional life exploring the truth about human existence and trying to present that truth on a stage. The booklet was entitled "Lines in the Palm of God's Hand."

The career of Jose Quintero was very much related to the plays of O'Neill. Back in 1956 Quintero "rediscov-

ered" O'Neill with his production of *The Iceman Cometh*
and rescued the great playwright's work from a kind of
limbo. The enormous success of *Iceman* was followed by
several Quintero-directed productions of O'Neill's plays.
However the bond between the two artists, who had
never met except through the text of O'Neill's plays, was
much deeper, in fact it seemed almost mystical. Quintero
wrote:

> "Since my first contact with O'Neill's work, I
> have experienced an emotional tie with it, a pro-
> found bond I cannot explain completely. My
> commitment to his work involves a deep love, as
> difficult to examine in its entirety as is the love of
> one human being for another. One continues to
> find valid, partial reasons for such a love, but the
> totality of the feeling, always intense, always an
> inseparable part of one, remains a mystical com-
> position, never fully exposed." [8]

That union between the two artists who never met fascinates me. Certainly if Jose could not explain it, I can't.
Both came from Roman Catholic backgrounds that
seemed to have an indelible influence on them. Both were
very spiritual people always searching and probing more
deeply into mystery. I think that in some ways art became
a kind of religion for each of them. A friend summarized
Jose's outlook as "Art was life; life was art, and there was
no separation." When as a college student I read *The
Iceman Cometh* I found the play repetitious but through
reading comments by Quintero I came to see that the repetition is never pointless but is rather like an orchestration
that reveals more and more deeply the themes of the play.

Jose wrote:

"My approach in directing *The Iceman Cometh* was different from that used in any play I had ever done. It had to be, for this was not built as an orthodox play. It resembles a complex musical form, with themes repeating themselves with slight variation, as melodies do in a symphony. It is a valid device, though O'Neill has often been criticized for it by those who do not see the strength and depth of meaning the repetition achieves."[9]

What most interests me about O'Neill's work and Quintero's work is the spiritual dimension that seems to have colored everything either did in the theater. This struck me especially during the memorial service for Quintero. Speaker after speaker mentioned the spiritual dimension of Jose's work. It seems clear that he thought of the theater as dealing with something sacred, as exploring ultimate meaning and celebrating what you took that ultimate meaning or mystery to be. Shortly after I learned of Jose's death, I said Mass for him. I feel a great debt to him for all he did to reveal to theatergoers the depth of what it means to be human.

Explicitly Religious Theater

My special interest in the theater is with plays which deal with ultimates: God, love and death. I am especially interested in theater that deals with these topics from an explicitly religious point of view. In our secular society there are not many opportunities to see explicitly religious theater pieces. To appear on a stage alone takes a special type of courage—and talent. Shows that involve only one performer present special problems in staging, but if done properly they can have tremendously powerful moments. I imagine actors and actresses relish an opportunity to be alone on a stage with only a text and their own skill at their disposal to entertain an audience. I can recall seeing a one-man show based on the life of Father Damien and another based on the life of Jesuit poet Gerard Manley Hopkins. I liked both shows, and I would love to see one based on the life of Cardinal John Henry Newman. One of the best I have ever seen was *Haunted by God* a play about Dorothy Day put on by Still Point. Reflecting about Still Point's existence has helped me to clarify my ideas about the relationship between theater and religion.

To understand what Still Point is, it helps to know something about its founder, Lisa Wagner. Approximately forty years of age, Lisa graduated from Emporia State College in Kansas. When she was a small child she dreamed of becoming an actress, and at 15 she wanted to become an ordained minister. While she was in her 20s, she struggled with how to put the two vocations together. Still Point is her solution.

For years Lisa worked at the charitable community called *L'Arche,* which is for developmentally disabled adults. After attending a Sunday Mass with one of the nuns from *L'Arche,* Lisa stayed after Mass to attend a seminar at which a Catholic priest spoke about Dorothy Day, about whom Lisa knew nothing. The priest told a story about Dorothy visiting a very disturbed woman in a mental institution. Though warned about the woman, who was in a padded cell, Dorothy still wanted to visit her. After sitting with the woman and calming her, Dorothy, upon leaving the padded cell, was asked by a staff member how she had accomplished this. She said "The other person in that room was Jesus." The anecdote led Lisa on a spiritual journey that has not ended but that has led her to study Dorothy Day's life and eventually led Lisa to create Still Point. Putting on Still Point productions has taken Lisa around the globe. Lisa took the title of her production group from a remark she heard a priest make about a "still point that is within each person where God lives that can't be touched." The dramas and performances seem to come from the still point in the creators' souls and reach out to speak to the still point in the souls of the audience. Lisa also teaches acting to developmentally disabled adults in Chicago. By teaching these adults acting, Lisa believes that she is helping them to reach out and help others. Indicating that she sees her theater work as a prayer, Lisa has said:

> "I really see performance as worship. The line between liturgy and theater is very foggy. There is something very special and beautiful and powerful about a live performance and that exchange that happens between the audience and you . . . I want people to start questioning themselves. 'What am I doing in my own life and how do I feel about people who have less than I do? How am I living out my own call? How much am I willing to sacrifice . . . Do I think about people with disabilities and how can I learn from them about how to fully live?' We really believe that will make a ripple effect in the world." [10]

I don't think that liturgy and theater are the same, but I think I understand what Lisa is doing. She is making her work a prayer. Anyone can do that with his or her work, but Lisa's work is very obviously spiritual and dealing with spiritual matters. Of course no matter what the spiritual possibilities of a work are, a person can miss those possibilities. I am not suggesting that every artist is aware that he or she is involved in something spiritual or in something that might lead to a religious experience. Years ago I interviewed an actor who was going to portray Jesus. The performer seemed to have no interest in the person of Jesus. It was just another part to play which he apparently approached the way he would approach any other part. I think that Lisa Wagner and others connected to Still Point are on to something important.

Haunted by God, a one-woman show created by Lisa, Robert Mc Clory and Paul Amandes and produced by Still Point Performing Arts and Call to Action, is one of the most spiritual plays I have ever seen. About Dorothy Day, the play could easily be put on in a parish. On the program that was available the evening I saw the play was the following quotation from Dorothy Day:

> "What we do is so little, but it is like the little boy with a few loaves and fishes. Christ took that little and increased it. He will do the rest. What we do is so little we may seem to be constantly failing. But so did he fail. He met with apparent failure on the cross. But unless the seed fall into the earth and die, there is no harvest. And why must we see results? Our work is to sow. Another generation will be reaping the harvest." [11]

I don't know whether I had ever read that quotation from Dorothy before the evening of the performance, but I have read similar quotations. The statement, like so many statements from her, expresses her profound faith and trust. Though Dorothy spent most of her life on the Bowery ministering to the poor, her witness has transcended the numbers of people to whom she was physically and personally present. People who never met her have been influenced by her. Priests, religious, laity and even many who are not Catholic have been inspired by Dorothy's life. Dorothy frequently pointed out that God has chosen the weak to confound the wise. Her own life, in one sense, was a small life confined to a small geographical area, but her influence was and is widespread. The play *Haunted by God* is a labor of love. It was created out of admiration for Dorothy.

So much of contemporary drama seems to deal with small subjects, and anything resembling an explicitly Christian drama is rare. When was the last time we saw a play dealing with a person's relationship with God? Can we even remember a play that dealt with a character whose life is modeled on the beatitudes? Those of us who are trying to follow Christ can be nourished by art that deals deeply with what we believe and cherish. A constant diet of art that is thoroughly secular not only does not nourish our faith, but can even exercise an adverse influence on our faith. *Haunted by God* deals with a woman who some think was the most influential American Catholic of the 20th century. The play can entertain us, instruct us and even inspire us.

For me a most distant memory that *Haunted by God* recalled was of myself as a young seminarian meeting

Dorothy Day. Though that first meeting took place fifty years ago, I still have a relatively vivid image of the first time I saw her. It was at the house of hospitality which was then on Chrystie Street in Manhattan. Dorothy had just been released by the police. She had been arrested because of her non-violent protests. As she entered the room, my heart jumped. I felt that I was seeing a saint. I still believe that. I cannot remember what I said to her, but even her physical appearance impressed me. She looked like a person who might be "haunted by God."

A Post-Christian Play

Peter Nichols' *The Passion Play* is a favorite of mine. The play deals with marital infidelity, and both the possibility and desirability of a marital life commitment. It also deals with the morality of adultery. James and Eleanor have been married, apparently happily, for 25 years. At the time that the play takes place, James is having an affair with a swinging '60s type, Kate, who seems to have no sexual morality at all. The passion seems to have left James' and Eleanor's marriage, but James' relationship with Kate is quite passionate.

What makes the play especially interesting in terms of the issues with which it deals is that James is a restorer of paintings and he is working on a painting of Christ. Eleanor is a music teacher with a fondness for church music. The dialogue is peppered with references to religion and art. Yet neither religion nor art provide James and Eleanor with any kind of vision of life that can serve as a support for their relationship. Clearly James and Eleanor inhabit a post-Christian world. In fact, James seems not only non-Christian but strongly anti-Christ. James views Christianity as against the body and sex.

Theatrically there are a number of interesting touches to the play. Both James and Eleanor have second selves, called Jim and Nell. For a time it seems that the second self is representing the subconscious or perhaps unspoken desires; but, as the play develops, that identification is not so easy to sustain. It becomes difficult to identify which self is the primary self or the more authentic self. My interpretation is that the confusion is deliberate on the part of Nichols. He is saying that both adultery and the complete absence of any meaningful religious faith make it difficult for a person to have an integrated life. Because reality is devoid of any ultimate meaning, it is difficult, if not impossible, to make a fulfilling life commitment. In reflecting on the "double identity" of the husband and the wife, I am reminded of a scene in an Ingmar Bergman film in which a person claims that recognition that there is no God led to the impression that reality had been split asunder. Nichols may be suggesting that without God nothing is firm or stable, what seemed reliable becomes uncertain and what seemed like solid ground appears like quicksand.

One of the most interesting aspects of James' character is that he admits that he does not know the meaning of the word "love." Describing him, Nell reports that "He says why call affection, lust, belief in God, patriotism, care for children, etcetera, by one word?" [12] At another point in the play, Eleanor reports about James' objections to her seeing a psychiatrist: "It smacks of church, he says, employing a professional to listen to our secrets. It means we have lost faith in human intercourse. Doctors for when the body

ails, yes, or the chemistry's unbalanced; but human questions need human answers."[13] In James, playwright
Nichols has given a brilliant example of the contemporary
secular humanist. While he rejects anything beyond the
human, he has missed completely the deepest dimension
of the human mystery. Losing faith in God may lead log-
ically to loss of faith in human intercourse.

The Passion Play raises all sorts of questions about religious faith and human love; and the play gives us a sear-
ing portrait of two people who recognize nothing superi-
or to themselves, and in that denial limit themselves
immensely. In the absence of any ultimates, Jim's view
that it is all right to have another sexual partner in addition to his wife makes some sense. If there are no
absolutes, then it would seem to be logical to do what
pleases you. Jim wants an adulterous affair. On what
grounds can this be denied him? The issues that *The
Passion Play* raises cause my mind to dance.

I think that *The Passion Play* dramatically illustrates
what living without God means. Because the married
people in Nichols' play have no passion for God, they
have no direction for their sexual passion. There is no ultimate meaning for their sexual passion. At one point in the
play, Jim, who is the alter ego for James, the restorer of
paintings who is working on a painting of the suffering
Christ, succinctly articulates his view of passion. He says:

"I've inspired love. That's my trouble. I'm an
unemotional man who's inspired a passion in
my partner. And I needn't tell you what passion
means? Suffering. Self-inflicted torture. Maso-
chism. All that's holy. Like that exquisite depic-

tion of a bleeding corpse that's waiting for me.

"By day, I'll patch up the blood and freshen the wounds where they've lost their brilliance over the years but every night . . ." [14]

He goes on to say that he will experience sexual pleasure every night through an adulterous relationship he has. Later, James says that he does not want anyone to die for love of him and Jim says that love is a terrible thing, at least the kind that kills, and so he suggests that they never use the word "love" again. I think that the play is suggesting that without the passion of Christ, sexual passion has no ultimate meaning and so if there is no sexual passion in a marriage, it is quite alright to seek sexual passion elsewhere. Also the lack of sexual passion in the married couple in the play is linked to their lack of belief in God. Contemporary theater that links human love to the existence of God, even if the link is only in the form of questions, is rare. Nichols' play is theatrically and thematically brilliant.

Probably my philosophy background makes the play especially interesting to me. The philosophical atmosphere that Peter Nichols sets for his characters is typical of a "Death of God" culture. In their struggle to make sense of their marriage and to deal with the infidelity of the husband, the two main characters have only their atheism to support them. It proves to be not enough. The two philosophers who kept coming to mind as I watched this brilliant dramatization of a contemporary marriage were Friedrich Nietzsche (1884-1900) and Jean Paul Sartre (1905-1980).

Drama as Anti-God

Nietzsche proclaimed the death of God in 19th century Europe. Of course he did not mean that there was a being, God, Who died. Nietzsche was an atheist. He meant that the idea of God, which once animated culture, which once was at the heart of literature, poetry, art, government, philosophy and all of life, was dead and that it no longer had any relevance for anyone, not even those who called themselves believers.

Nietzsche saw the implications of this very clearly and believed that once people became aware of "God's death" they would realize that they were adrift without any anchor or support. They would realize that they no longer had anything substantial on which to base their lives. I think that much of what Nietzsche said about 19th century Europe could be applied to contemporary life in the United States. Though surveys suggest that many people believe in God, we do live in a post-Judeo Christian culture. Today religious belief does not directly animate politics, literature, theater, art, philosophy, poetry or film. Though I have a strong interest in film and theater, I usually cannot find films or plays that speak explicitly, meaningfully and deeply to my religious faith. The characters in Nichols' play live in a culture that resembles the death of God culture described by Nietzsche.

I teach Sartre's play *The Flies* each year at St. John's University in Jamaica, New York, in a course on existentialism and the play has a special importance for me. Sartre uses the story to dramatize his atheism, and I think a study of the play can call theists to correct some of the false notions that they may have about God. In what I think is the most dramatic scene in *The Flies* Orestes is confronted by Zeus, who in Sartre's version is a stand-in for Sartre's understanding of Western philosophy's image of God. Zeus is scolding Orestes because he does not show the proper respect for Zeus. Earlier in the play, Zeus has warned the new king that they had better be wary of Orestes because he is a free man, and Zeus points out that free men have no use for gods or kings. Talking to Orestes Zeus says:

> "Orestes, I created you, and I created all things ... See those planets wheeling on their appointed way, never swerving never clashing. It was I who ordained their courses, according to the laws of justice. Hear the music of the spheres, that vast mineral hymn of praise, sounding and resounding to the limits of the firmament. It is my work that living things increase and multiply, each according to his kind. I have ordained that man shall always beget man, and dog give birth to dog. It is my work that the tides with their innumerable tongues creep up to lap the sand and draw back at the appointed hour. I make the plants grow, and my breath fans round the earth the yellow clouds of pollen. You are not in your own home, intruder; you are a foreign body in the world, like a splinter in flesh, or a poacher in his lordship's forest. For the world is good; I made it according to my will, and I am Goodness. . . ." [15]

Orestes replies that Zeus is the god of the ordered universe, but he is not the god of free men. Sartre is expressing his view that human freedom means that there can be no God. For Sartre, if there were a god, that would mean that God would be running everything, and a human person could not be free. But Sartre insists that we are free, and so there cannot be a God.

Sartre once gave a talk to French communists in which he tried to make clear what it meant to be an atheist. He told them that being an atheist did not mean killing the Judeo-Christian God and then turning something else—money or power or pleasure or fame—into a God. Sartre insisted that being an atheist meant having no gods. Being an atheist meant being adrift and alone in the universe. For me Sartre's vision of the human person is that everything in us is directed toward God but the joke is that there is no God and so reality is absurd. Sartre's *The Flies* and especially the conversation between Zeus and Orestes dramatizes what Nietzsche called "the death of God." Unfortunately, for religious believers much of American theater over the last seventy years or so has dramatized human existence without direct reference to the divine.

Sartre's particular brand of atheism can call theists to purify their images of God so that we might see that our freedom is not decreased by God's presence in our lives but rather increased by God's presence in our lives. I have come to believe that the holiest people are also the freest people.

Whether it be through Arthur Miller's and Tennessee Williams' profound insights into human nature or the remnants of abandoned Catholicism in O'Neill, or explicitly religious drama such as Still Point produces or the explicitly irreligious drama of Nichols and Sartre, theater can serve as a magnet toward God.

Questions for Reflection

1. Why do you think some artists make art their religion? What do you think is the difference between art and religion?
2. What does Pope John Paul II mean when he says that "art remains a kind of bridge to religious experience" even when a culture and the Church are far apart?
3. In what sense, if any, is *The Death of a Salesman* a religious play?
4. How is Eugene O'Neill's Catholicism present in *A Moon for the Misbegotten?* In any of his other plays?
5. What do you think of the "apostolate" of Still Point?
6. Can a post-Christian play such as *The Passion Play* nourish religious faith? If it can, how?
7. Can an anti-God play such as *The Flies* nourish Christian faith? If so, how?

---

[1] *A Streetcar Named Desire* (New York: Penguin, 1947), p. 96.

[2] John Paul II, *Letter to Artists,* p. 4.

[3] Croswell Bowen, the "The Black Irishman" in *O'Neill and His Plays: Four Decades of Criticism,* edited by Oscar Cargil, N. Bryllion and William J. Fisher (New York University Press, 1961), pp. 64-65.

[4] Louis Sheaffer, *O'Neill: Son and Artist* (Boston: Little, Brown and Company, 1973), p. 306.

[5] Edward Shaughnessy, *Down the Nights and Down the Days; Eugene O'Neill's Catholic Sensibility,* (University of Notre Dame, 1996), pp. 36-37.

[6] *The New York Times,* Online Edition, March 20, 2000, p. 2.

[7] *O'Neill and His Plays, op. cit.,* pp. 125, 126.

[8] As yet unpublished autobiography "And That Was That" in *Lines in the Palm of God's Hand.* A tribute to Jose Quintero, edited by Joseph Arnold and John Brugaletta (Southwest Press, 1999), p. 7.

[9] Jose Quintero, "Postcripts to a Journey" in *Lines in the Palm of God's Hand,* Ibid., pp. 4-5

[10] *Chicago Tribune,* Section 8, July 14, 1999, pp.1, 7.

[11] Dorothy Day, "Ends and Purposes" in *The Catholic Worker,* February 1940, p. 7.

[12] Peter Nichols, *The Passion Play* (London: Eyre Methuen, 1981), p. 82.

[13] Ibid., p. 83.

[14] Ibid., p. 88.

[15] Jean Paul Sartre, "The Flies" in *No Exit and Three Other Plays* (New York: Vintage Books, 1948), pp. 119-120.

4

Meditation and the Medium of Literature

"The fiction writer presents mystery through manners, grace through nature, but when he finishes there always has to be left over the sense of Mystery which cannot be accounted for by any human formula." [1]

—Flannery O'Connor

Storytelling Matters

In the Preface of his book *A Stay Against Confusion: Essays on Faith and Fiction*, novelist Ron Hansen makes some important points about stories. Looking back on his childhood, Hansen thinks that churchgoing and religion played a big role in leading him to his vocation as a writer. He notes:

"Looking back on my childhood now, I find that churchgoing and religion were in good part the origin of my vocation as a writer, for along with Catholicism's feast for the senses, its ethical concerns, its insistence on seeing God in all things and the high status it gave to Scripture, drama and art, there was a connotation in Catholicism's liturgies that storytelling mattered.

Each Mass was a narrative steeped in meaning and metaphor, helping the faithful not only to remember the past but to make it present here and now and to bind ourselves into a sharing group so that, ideally, we could continue the public ministry of Jesus in our world." [2]

I think that Hansen's insight that there is a connotation in Catholic liturgy that storytelling matters is extremely important. Stories are what enable us to hold our life together, and not only to hold it together but to make of it something beautiful. Catholicism's insistence that God is everywhere reveals that there are no small or insignificant stories, that every person's story is being written by that person but also by the Holy Spirit. People are co-authors with God.

Hansen points out that writing not only gives form and meaning to the sometimes disorderly life of the writer, but it also gives the author the opportunity to reveal himself or herself, to form a communion with readers. An author gives readers a share in his or her life and perhaps that sharing illuminates for readers their own lives. That has certainly been my experience as a reader of fiction.

Hansen suggests that by reading attentively we can connect our lives with those of fictional characters and that by choosing ethically and emotionally as they do or even in contradistinction to them, we can enter more deeply into a spiritual realm that may help us to see the similarity and dissimilarities between a fictional character and ourselves. Eventually this may help us to become more aware of God as the creator of our existence. Once again this has been my experience in reading Catholic novels. Not only do fictional characters become more real, but God can become more real.

I had a friend who was a voracious reader. He loved to read history, but he did not like to read fiction. He thought of it as untrue. Of course, fiction is not true in the way that history is true, but it is true in a very important sense. Great fiction tells us about the meaning of freedom, the meaning of love and perhaps the meaning of God. It can be said that fiction is at least as true as history if we are talking about essential meanings. History tells us what events occurred, but fiction can tell us about the meaning of the events. Great fiction can reveal us to ourselves in profound ways, can help us to see the truth about ourselves in new and deeper ways.

Though I have been saying Mass for more than forty years, Hansen's description of Mass as "a narrative steeped in meaning and metaphor" gave me a slightly new way of thinking about the Mass. At each Mass we tell Jesus' story. In fact, we act out that story, and we hope that this action will help us to write our own stories more meaningfully and more beautifully. We don't just look back on Jesus' story, but we look to the future to continue his story in our stories.

There is a collection of essays taken from the first 75 years of Commonweal magazine entitled *Commonweal Confronts the Century: Liberal Convictions, Catholic Tradition.* In the collection there is a review by Evelyn Waugh of Graham Greene's novel *The Heart of the Matter.* The essay, which was first published in the issue of Commonweal dated July 16, 1948, is entitled *"Felix Culpa?"* When I discovered the essay, I figured I was in for a double treat, an essay written by one of my favorite novelists, about a novel by my favorite novelist. The essay did not disappoint me.

One of the first thoughts I had while reading Waugh's review was that I had forgotten that English could be written so beautifully. Back in high school my Jesuit English teacher raved about Waugh as a stylist. At that time I had to take his word that Waugh's writing was exceptional, but even this brief essay reveals Waugh's mastery of the language. Even when I disagree with what he is saying, I find his way of expressing it special. I wonder if there is anyone writing this well today. The following are the two opening paragraphs of the review:

> "Of Mr. Graham Greene alone among contemporary writers one can say without affectation that his breaking silence with a new serious novel is a literary 'event'. It is eight years since the publication of *The Power and the Glory*. During that time he has remained inconspicuous and his reputation has grown huge. We have had leisure to reread his earlier books and to appreciate the gravity and intensity which underlie their severe modern surface. More than this, the spirit of the time has begun to catch up with them.
>
> "The artist, however aloof he holds himself, is always and specially the creature of the zeitgeist: however formally antique his tastes, he is in spite of himself in the advance guard. Men of affairs stumble far behind."[3]

Waugh's comments about the artist being "in the advance guard" reminds me of psychologist Rollo May's insight that the artist often feels earlier than anyone what becomes an emotional problem for a later age. No matter how the great artist secludes himself or herself, the artist is out ahead of the rest of us. Greene was a great artist. In relation to *The Heart of the Matter* and Greene's foresight, Waugh points out that the question he most heard from agnostics was not about some pious belief or even about some moral teaching but rather, "Do you believe in hell?"

The central problem of *The Heart of the Matter* centers around whether the main character, Scobie, because of his suicide, goes to hell. In the novel the plot so develops that Scobie sees his own suicide as the only way he can avoid hurting either his wife or his mistress. There is a scene in the novel in which, in order to avoid hurting his wife, he accompanies her to Mass and receives the Eucharist, even though he believes he is committing a sacrilege and assuring hell as his destiny. When he eventually commits suicide, he does it out of love. So the question becomes "Is Scobie's suicide an act of despair or an act of love? Does it send him to hell or to heaven?"

I think Greene's preoccupations are contained in the frontispiece of the novel which Greene took from the French poet Charles Peguy. The statement by the poet, which Greene leaves in French, says that the sinner is at the very heart of Christianity, that no one understands Christianity as well as the sinner, unless it be the saint.

The theological paradox in *The Heart of the Matter* is that Scobie may be saved in spite of his suicide or perhaps even because of it. At the end of the novel Scobie's wife is discussing her husband's death with a priest, Father Rank. She says to the priest that because her husband committed suicide there wasn't any point in praying for him. Then Greene has the following dialogue:

"Father Rank . . . said furiously, 'For goodness' sake, Mrs. Scobie, don't imagine you—or I— know a thing about God's mercy.

'The Church says . . .'

'I know what the Church says. The Church knows all the rules. But it doesn't know what goes on in a single human heart.' "[4]

I first read *The Heart of the Matter* in the mid-1950s and loved it. Through the years other Greene novels appealed to me more, but about two years ago I reread it and was reminded how good the novel is. Eventually Greene came to dislike it, but I think it is exceptionally good. In his review Waugh claims that only a Catholic could understand the novel and that even some Catholics will misunderstand it, those who think that it is the function of the Catholic writer to issue advertising brochures setting out the advantages of membership in the Church.

Waugh writes "To them this profoundly reverent book will seem a scandal." The novel did fulfill Waugh's prediction that it would lead to controversy. Perhaps Waugh has the final and best word about the novel. He writes that the answer to Scobie's problem is in the mind of God alone, "the reconciliation of perfect justice with perfect mercy." That may be the best summary statement about *The Heart of the Matter*.

Literature and Theology

I once heard moral theologian Sister Anne E. Patrick, SNJM, give a stimulating and provocative lecture entitled

"Imaginative Literature and Moral Theology." One of the main points that Sister Anne stressed was that a problem with moral theology is that it has tended to overlook or forget the mystery of God. Sister believes that imaginative literature can help us to be aware that in theology we are dealing with the mystery of God and so we must avoid the tendency to think that we can completely understand human beings or their actions.

In pointing out the special help that imaginative literature can provide for those who do theology, Sister used a marvelous phrase. She said art is a "calculated trap for meditation." I love that phrase. All art calls us to stop and to think. Literature can call us to see things differently, to question our too narrow opinions, to open ourselves to what is new and different. In trying to illustrate how literature can cause us to meditate and be aware of the mystery of God, Sister used various literary works, one of which was Graham Greene's masterpiece *The Power and the Glory*.

In *The Power and the Glory* we have a whiskey priest who has fathered an illegitimate child. By our customary standards we would not think of this man as a very good priest. Yet Greene once again presents a theological paradox. The priest, though he believes that he is going to hell because of his serious sins, lays down his life for his flock. In fact this very weak, frail vessel of clay becomes a martyr. I think Greene is suggesting that the "whiskey priest" is a saint.

Once again, the artist, in this case a novelist, causes us to pause and reflect on the mystery of God's infinite mercy and God's strange providential ways. I am reminded of St. Augustine looking back on his sins and seeing that God used even his sins to draw Augustine closer to Himself. *The Power and the Glory* and other great novels are "a calculated trap for meditation."

Stories are absolutely necessary for our conception of ourselves. If we don't have a narrative then we don't have a sense of self. The great stories have formed us and each of us is writing his or her own story within what we understand to be the story of creation or the narrative of the human race. Without a sense of a story bigger than ourselves that includes ourselves, we would have no sense of who we are. Today the way in which many once thought of themselves no longer speaks to them. The narrative that once illumined their experience, motivated and inspired them, no longer speaks deeply, if at all, to them. Many feel they are adrift. There are Catholics whose prior understanding of being Catholic no longer illuminates or inspires. A deeper, more encompassing story may be required. My faith tells me that there is a depth to the story of Christ that can successfully encompass both the story of priesthood and the story of Catholicism. One of the strong forces that have put a stress on people's understanding of the Christian story is secular or atheistic humanism. I do not believe that we can overemphasize the influence of this philosophy.

Thinking back on my own academic and intellectual life, I am surprised at what little importance I gave to the imagination for much of my life. My own undergraduate training in philosophy made me a little suspicious of the imagination. I thought the imagination was related to the emotions which I also suspected. What I wanted was pure intellectual thinking unencumbered by images. Even as I write this I am smiling. How wrong could one person be? I now think that imagination is extremely important. Images can have an enormously powerful impact on us. One crisis in the Catholic church at this time is the absence of a Catholic imagination in many Catholics. The imaginations of many Catholics have become secularized. The culture has brainwashed us.

Stories of The Divine Presence

Looking through the table of contents of a recently published collection of short stories edited by Brother Michel Bettigole, OSF, *Tales of God: A Treasury of Great Short Stories for the Catholic Family,* I felt as though I was meeting some old friends. There are at least two stories in Michel's collection that had a profound impact on me when I was young, and there are several authors whom I look upon as companions in my journey through life. I can only guess how much my conscience has been formed by the literature that I have read.

In his preface Brother Michel writes:

"Great literature has always played a significant role in the oral and religious education of the young. Men and women of letters and pedagogy have continuously stressed the role of appropriate reading and storytelling for the proper inculcation of religious and spiritual values. In every generation parents, grandparents, and teachers have told tales of faith to the young and thus passed on to them those eternal values that are exemplified in the stories and legends of heroes and saints. It is primarily through stories and other imaginative activities that young people become aware of the divine universe that surrounds them and learn to distinguish between right and wrong, good and evil."[5]

I agree completely with that statement, and I wish that all teachers believed in the power of story to form people. Though my memory is a bit shaky concerning my grandmother, I have some recollection of her telling me stories. In my home, when I was a student in grammar school, a regular evening activity for my mother, father, sister and me was reading. I can recall books that were important to me when I was a child, and I suspect that they had a profound effect on my imagination.

I don't think that Brother Michel is exaggerating when he identifies stories as one of the primary realities that introduce young people to the divine universe and help them to distinguish between what is right and what is wrong, between what is good and what is evil. Of course at what age a person reads a story can be crucial. Young people are impressionable. The two stories in Michel's collection that had a profound influence when I read them "at the right moment" in my life are J.F. Powers' "The Trouble" and Graham Greene's "The Hint of an Explanation." I read "The Trouble" when I was a junior at a Jesuit High School and I read Greene's story when I was a seminarian studying for the priesthood.

Powers' story impressed on me the evil of racial prejudice and especially how racial prejudice is just not permitted for Catholics. My guess is that the Jesuits and dedicated laymen (there were no female teachers in Jesuit high school back in those days) indicated the evil of racial prejudice to us in many ways; but what is most clear in my memory is Powers' story. There was great enthusiasm among my classmates when we read and discussed "The Trouble." With extremely powerful images, Powers made his point that a serious 'trouble' among Catholics was racial prejudice.

"The Trouble" is about a race riot in a big city in this country. Blacks are being attacked by whites and in turn are attacking whites. The story is told by a small black child who is watching the riot from the window of his family's apartment. His mother has been attacked by whites and is brought into the apartment seriously injured. A white man, who during the riot has been attacking blacks, seeks shelter in the apartment in order to escape some blacks who are pursuing him. The black family sends for the parish priest to administer the last rites to the mother. As great short story writers are able to do, Powers weaves into the story important insights into human nature. The story is especially powerful in its criticism of racism.

At one point in the story, the frightened white man, who even in the apartment reveals his racism, says to the priest that he would like to leave with him, thinking that being with the priest would protect him during the riot. The priest remarks "You won't be the first one to hide behind a Roman collar." At another point in the story, the Catholic, trying to defend himself, says to the priest, "I'm a Catholic, too, Father." The priest responds "That's the trouble."

In my seminary education I learned a great deal about the mystery of the Eucharist. My years in the seminary coincided with a great liturgical revival that was happening in this country. When I was studying sacraments and liturgy, I received many wonderful insights from professors and books. I think that it was a fairly common custom for seminarians to visit the Blessed Sacrament four or five times a day in addition to required attendance at prayer in the chapel. Yet in my memory Graham Greene's "The Hint of an Explanation" holds a special place. I can recall my excitement the first time I read it. In the unique way that a great storyteller has, Greene dramatically made Christ's presence in the Eucharist the center of his story. I wonder if there is anything more powerful than stories. They have a special power to engage us and to influence us. If you want a child's attention, tell him or her a story. If you want an adult's attention, tell him or her a story. Most homilists and teachers can testify that when they are telling stories, the attention and interest of their listeners are obvious.

At the beginning of "The Hint of an Explanation" two men meet on a train. They strike up a conversation and it turns out that one is a believer and the other isn't. The believer decides to tell about something in his childhood that might give the unbeliever the hint of an explanation as to why he believes. He tells about being an altar boy in a largely non-Catholic village. One day while walking toward home after serving Mass, he is invited into a bakery shop and the baker whose name is Blacker shows him a magnificent set of electric trains and tells him he can come in any day and play with them. One day the baker says the boy can have them if he does the baker a favor. He wants the boy to bring him a consecrated host from Mass so that the baker can study the bread. The boy, who is ten years old at the time, is sufficiently intelligent to know that the baker wants to desecrate the host. Desiring the trains, the boy takes the communion wafer from his mouth at Mass and puts it into his pocket in a piece of newspaper, but then feeling guilty does not go to the bakery shop but goes home. Blacker follows him and stands outside his bedroom window begging for the host which the boy has placed on a chair in his room. The believer in the train who is narrating the event from his childhood, says to the agnostic:

"I was . . . haunted by the presence of God there on the chair. The Host had always been to me—well, the Host. I knew theoretically, as I have said, what I had to believe, but suddenly, as someone whistled in the road outside, whistled secretively, knowingly, to me, I knew that this which I had beside my bed was something of infinite value—something a man would pay for with his whole peace of mind, something that was so hated one could love it as one loves an outcast or a bullied child . . . There was only one place where He was safe. I couldn't separate the Host from the paper, so I swallowed both." [6]

In his preface to his collection *Tales of God* Brother Michel writes:

"In his recent 'Letter to artists' (April 1999), Pope John Paul II stressed the importance of the visual, literary, and performing arts in the life of faith. He pointed out that it is through the arts that religious truths are made tangible: 'making perceptible . . . the world of the spirit, of the invisible, of God.' In emphasizing the critical role that the arts have on the development of the moral imagination and the formation of conscience, Pope John Paul II was echoing the insights of philosophers and theologians throughout the ages who have always stressed the role of the arts in the formation of a mind attuned to the Good, the True, and the Beautiful."[7]

We believe that God is the creator of all and that everything to some extent mirrors God's existence. Creatures are like messages from God. I suppose that some saints and poets are more aware of this than the rest of us. I think that the Pope is reminding us of the importance that art and culture can play in our expression of faith and in our grasp of the faith. Great stories can help us to be more sensitive, to be more aware of the mysteries that surround us, to be more aware of the mystery of God.

The good, the true, and the beautiful are everywhere, but storytellers can make them more evident for us. Great storytellers can reveal the true, the good and the beautiful. Their stories can comfort us, challenge us and inspire us. Reading great stories can help us to "write" our own stories better. Each person is co-creating with God the story of his or her life. The meaning or lack of meaning that our lives may seem to have at any given moment is due to the way our story is going. Some days everything seems wonderful, other days nothing seems wonderful. I think that great stories usually point at least implicitly to the mystery of God.

We are surrounded by stories, our own and those of others, and how we react to those stories determines to a large extent who we are. Our stories are the result of our relationships and of our interaction with others and their stories. It can almost be said that a person is his or her story. In his preface to *Tales of God* Brother Michel writes:

"Ours is a post-Christian age whose literature glorifies the secular. The sensuality, materialism, and utilitarianism that mark so much of present-day adult writing finds its reflection in modern tales for children and adolescents. One finds in so much contemporary writing stories that exalt material success and fame. Rarely does the reader find a well-written story that portrays the world of the spirit and the life of grace. The lack of the divine in so much modern literature, its utter denial of things of the spirit and spirituality, has resulted in a shrinking of the imagination and a closing of the mind for both adults and children. The universe of people and things has been tied down to the purely measurable and functional instead of being open to the unseen but all so real worlds of the eternal and the miraculous." [8]

There is a great deal in that paragraph that calls for serious reflection. Though I wish that Michel were wrong, I am afraid that he is basically right in his assessment of the contemporary scene. There is no doubt that ours is a post-Christian age and that the secular is glorified. This is not an easy age for religious believers to nourish their faith. Depending on how secular a person becomes, the world of faith will seem less and less real. The fading of the world of faith from the center of our consciousness can be a slow, subtle, almost unnoticeable process. What makes me angry is that the world that is being presented to children and adolescents is so narrow and ultimately so false.

Psychiatrist Victor Frankl claimed that a totally secular culture could cause people to be emotionally ill because it did not speak to their religious yearnings and deep religious needs. I find this a fascinating idea and it fits in with my own philosophy of person. Put very simply, we are made for God, we are magnetized toward God, and a culture that does not nourish the basic direction that our lives should take might cause emotional problems. Though I am not competent to know whether Frankl was correct in his psychological indictment of a thoroughly secular culture, I do know that a totally secular culture does shrink people's imagination. It leaves out what is most real, what is at the depth of the human person, what is at the basis of all reality. I believe that the secularist's view of reality is woefully inadequate. This is not to say that there are not secularists who are exceptionally moral people, perhaps much holier than many of us Christians, but the vision of reality and of human existence that the secularist presents leaves out the divine, and that means that it leaves out the most important dimension of the human person. One way of combating the secularist vision, which seems to predominate in so much of contemporary culture, is to make available stories that have a religious dimension. Such stories can wake us up to what is most important about us.

Years ago a priest whom I greatly admire painted for me the problem that plagues contemporary teachers of religion on all levels of education. He said that a person teaching religion could make the best lesson plan, conduct the most marvelous class, and yet the impact that the teaching would have on students would be very slight because as soon as the students leave the classroom, there is nothing in our secular culture that would support or nourish what the teacher had taught. This is a little frightening, but unfortunately I think the priest's assessment of contemporary culture and of the problems that face teachers of religion is still basically accurate. I have total confidence that the Christian story has the power to transform people's consciousness and to change people's hearts but people have to come in contact with that story.

Literature and Conversion

I think that I first came across the idea of intellectual conversion as distinct from other types of conversion through the thought of the great 20th century Catholic theologian, Bernard Lonergan. It certainly was through Lonergan that I came upon the discussion of the differences among intellectual, moral and religious conversions. The analysis that Lonergan gave of the various types of conversion made a great deal of sense to me and illuminated for me my experience of people dramatically redirecting their lives. Lonergan's insights into conversion have been on my mind as I have been thinking about the importance of stories in our lives.

Every person has a horizon of meanings that are real to him or her. We might say that every person lives within a world of meaning, and by "world" I wish to indicate a network or set of meanings that are real to that person. For example, the meanings of Catholic theology are part of my horizon or world but the meanings of calculus are not real to me. I have never taken a course in calculus and I do not have even the slightest understanding of calculus. An intellectual conversion takes place when a person radically changes his or her horizon or world of meaning. For example, imagine a person who has believed in Marxism but then rejects Karl Marx's vision of reality and embraces St. Thomas Aquinas' view of reality. Such a person would have undergone an intellectual conversion. Or imagine a Christian who becomes an agnostic. To go from Christian faith to agnostic faith would involve an intellectual conversion.

A moral conversion indicates that a person has changed his or her way of living. Imagine an individual who in the past had habitually committed sins of the flesh. When that person decides to make a life commitment in marriage and is faithful to that commitment, a moral conversion has taken place. An individual's lifestyle has taken a new direction. Though I tend to think of moral conversions as following from intellectual conversions, that is not necessarily always the process. A person can experience an intellectual conversion but not change his or her lifestyle. A person can experience a moral conversion without an intellectual conversion preceding that change of direction in the person's life.

Lonergan described a religious conversion as a person falling in love with God. Once again I tend to think of a religious conversion as following a moral conversion which came about after an intellectual conversion. This seemed to be the order of conversions in the life of the great St. Augustine, at least as he reported his conversions in *The Confessions*. The great saint was a Manichean for a time but eventually experienced an intellectual conversion to Christianity. But just because he believed in Christ did not immediately move Augustine to change his way of living. For a time after his intellectual conversion, Augustine continued to visit prostitutes. Eventually he began to live a Christian moral life. After this moral conversion, Augustine chose to be totally committed to Christ and seems to have had what Lonergan called a religious conversion.

Great literature can call people to conversion. That there is literature that can call readers to an intellectual conversion to Christianity is a very good thing. Most contemporary literature would not seem to do that. How a person thinks will eventually, I believe, have an impact on how a person lives, and how a person lives will either point that person toward or away from God. In my philosophy classes at St. John's University, I am calling my students to an intellectual conversion. I am inviting them to embrace some very important truths about self, neighbor and God. I think that this is my role, my mission as a professor of philosophy. At liturgy in my preaching, I am calling people to all three conversions, intellectual, moral and religious.

Literature has the power to change our lives. My opinion is that one book can change the life of someone. This may not happen often, but it does seem to happen. Richard Gilman in his *Faith, Sex and Mystery*[9] reports that he stayed up one night reading Etienne Gilson's *The Spirit of Medieval Philosophy* and that by morning he believed in Catholicism.

Whether or not one book can change anyone's life, I have no doubt that a constant diet of the same type of reading has to have some impact on the life of the reader. When we read a piece of literature, we are allowing the author to present to us, with whatever skill the author possesses, the vision of reality that he or she has. Depending on the author's ability, the piece of literature will have a strong or weak influence on us.

I know that reading good literature has fallen on bad times. Perhaps there are too many distractions, perhaps many young people have not yet experienced the joy of reading. I find that even bright college students do not seem to have developed the habit of reading for pleasure. All educators have to be concerned about this. I know that in the courses I teach I have to resist pressure from some students to cut the amount of assigned reading. They tell me that I have a reputation for demanding too much reading. Though I listen to the criticism, I always have to weigh it against my belief that college is a golden moment in people's lives, an opportunity to read that they probably will never have again. I am always hoping that once someone falls in love with reading, he or she will be hooked for life.

Literature and the Vision of Faith

I first came upon the name of Flannery O'Connor in the mid-fifties when I was a seminarian. A terrific essay by O'Connor appeared in *America* magazine and several seminarians were very impressed by her ideas about the vocation of the Catholic writer. None of my friends, except one, had ever heard of her. He had read one of her stories and claimed that there was nothing in it that might be described as "Catholic." I found this incredible. Years later, when I started reading O'Connor's stories, I understood why my friend erroneously thought that the story he had read had nothing to do with Catholicism. The Catholic dimension of O'Connor's writing eludes some people, even some professional critics.

The essay that appeared in *America* is, along with some other terrific essays by her, in O'Connor's *Mystery and Manners*. [10] Anyone who reads this book should have a very good sense of the Catholic vision of Flannery O'Connor. The task will be to see that vision in her fiction.

I describe detecting the Catholic vision in O'Connor's fiction as a "task" because of my experience in having friends and students read them. I have one friend who loved several Catholic novels I gave her to read but when I gave her my favorite O'Connor short story, "A Good Man Is Hard to Find," she hated it, could see nothing Catholic in it and could not figure out why I asked her to read it. But confusion is not limited to my friends and students. In a collection of stories that included "A Good Man Is Hard to Find" the suggested questions for discussion about the story revealed that the editor who composed the questions had missed completely the religious dimension of the story. Yet the distinguished critic Alfred Kazin claimed a few years ago that the one 20th century American religious writer who will withstand the test of time will be O'Connor.

In an essay entitled "The Church and the Fiction Writer" in *Mystery and Manners* O'Connor states succinctly what distinguishes the writer who has a Catholic vision from the secularist:

"A belief in fixed dogma cannot fix what goes on in life or blind the believer to it. It will, of course, add a dimension to the writer's observation which many cannot, in conscience, acknowledge exists, but as long as what they 'can' is present in the work, they cannot claim that any freedom has been denied the artist. A dimension taken away is one thing, a dimension added is another; and what the Catholic writer and reader will have to remember is that the reality of the added dimension will be judged in a work of fiction by the truthfulness and wholeness of the natural events presented. If the Catholic writer hopes to reveal mysteries, he will have to do it by describing truthfully what he sees from where he is." [11]

For about twenty years I have been meeting with a group of nine priests in a book discussion club. We have talked about more than fifty books. In the group there are experts on the Church's social teaching, professional theologians, philosophers, and a former English teacher. There are a couple of pastors, retired pastors and a bishop. One of the most provocative discussions we have had was on Alice McDermott's prize-winning novel *Charming Billy*.

The first thing that struck me about Mc Dermott's novel was her ability to capture the way that Irish-Americans of a particular generation spoke. She captures the speech patterns and indeed the thought patterns of an entire group of Irish Catholics. My guess is that readers of Irish descent will recognize either their parents or grand-children, uncles or aunts, cousins or neighbors in the novel. My experience with great novels is that they are able to capture you right away and draw you into their story. McDermott quickly draws the reader into the Irish-American culture of her characters. Not only is Billy charming but all the characters in the story are great company. As I was reading *Charming Billy* the first writer who came to my mind was James Joyce. Not that Alice McDermott has reached Joyce's stature, but both, as some of my Irish friends might say, "have a way with words." Both have written prose that at times sounds like poetry. Though not yet Joyce, McDermott is an exceptionally talented novelist.

The plot of *Charming Billy* centers around Billy Lynch. A lovable alcoholic, Billy has drunk himself to death at the age of 60. The novel opens with those who attend Billy's funeral Mass gathering in a restaurant in Queens for lunch. In her setting of the scene and in the dialogue she gives her characters at the luncheon, McDermott reveals her exceptional skills as a storyteller and immediately has our attention. The rest of the novel recounts the life of Billy through the memories of those who knew him and especially those who loved him. I think that every priest in our group who has an Irish heritage knew someone in his family like Billy Lynch, someone with an attractive personality, perhaps exceptionally gifted, who just could not handle alcohol.

At the start of our discussion, the priests had different reactions to McDermott's story. One priest found the book pessimistic but he was in the minority. All of us were especially interested in the frequent allusions to faith, both Billy's and others'. We all knew that whatever else this novel is about, it is also about faith. I have heard that McDermott was surprised that critics, even those who praised the book, did not deal with the subject of faith in their critiques. When asked about the themes of the novel, McDermott commented "I thought it was about faith."

During the hour and a half that the priests discussed the novel each priest had an opportunity to offer his ideas. At one point, one of the priests said "I think it is about the communion of saints." I think he was right. In addition to being a very big drinker Billy seems to be a person of very strong faith. Several times during the novel his faith is referred to by other people, and at least one character talks about Billy's holiness. In one scene in the novel, Billy, while drunk, calls his best friend and talks about the faith. Billy says:

> "Death is a terrible thing . . . our Lord knew it was terrible. Why would he have shed his own blood if death wasn't terrible? . . . You know what makes a mockery of the crucifixion? . . . You know what makes it pointless? Anyone saying that death is just an ordinary thing, an ordinary part of life. It happens; you reconcile yourself; you go on. Anyone saying that is saying our Lord's coming was to no avail. . . . Why do we need the Redemption?. . . If death isn't terrible. If we're reconciled? Why do we need heaven and hell? It makes no difference. If death doesn't trouble us, the injustice of it, then we don't need heaven or hell, do we? It might as well be a lie." [12]

The speech by Billy suggests something of the complexity of McDermott's novel. Billy, while he is making the speech on the phone, is extremely drunk, yet everything he says makes sense. It almost seems as though Billy's faith is somehow linked to his alcoholism. I don't mean that his faith is an alcoholic delusion but that his romantic approach to life seems to be related to his faith and also to his drinking. At one point in the novel, one of Billy's friends says that Billy believed that life was poetry and prayer and that other people knew that Billy was wrong. Was he? I think he was correct.

One of the themes of this exceptionally well-written book is that each person is a mystery, that no person should be reduced to any one aspect of his or her personality, that each person is more than any single personal characteristic. I refer to the reducing of persons to some function or role or personal characteristic as the "nothing but" approach. We observe a great deal of this type of reductionism in our society when we hear people say things like "He's nothing but black," or "She is nothing but a professional student," or "He is nothing but a janitor." McDermott's novel is very humorous in its depiction of some Irish American mores, but ultimately is a serious depiction of a person who cannot and should not be easily categorized.

Billy is an alcoholic who drinks himself to death by the age of 60 but that is not all he is. He seems to be a person of deep faith and at least some characters in the novel think of him as very holy. What are we to make of charming Billy? That is the question that stayed with me after I finished reading the novel. Thinking about Billy Lynch, I recalled a lengthy argument I had more than forty-five years ago with a classmate in the seminary. The two of us had seen Elia Kazan's classic film *A Tree Grows in Brooklyn* based on Betty Smith's novel. In the film, James Dunne plays an Irish alcoholic, Johnny Nolan, the head of a very poor family, which is poor at least partly because of his drinking. Dunne, who won an Academy Award for best supporting actor for his performance, is absolutely magnificent.

Some who come from an Irish Catholic background may have had personal experiences with men such as Johnny. The character reminds me of one of my uncles. Johnny Nolan, though not well educated, is intelligent, a poet and a dreamer. At one point in the film, one character says something like, "When Johnny said hello to you it was as though he was giving you a gift. It just made you feel good all over." I recall someone telling me how she felt good all day because she had a chance meeting with my uncle on the street. Were both characters capable of Irish blarney? Of course, but there was more than that to them. There was a marvelous loving approach to people and a sense that life with all its sufferings was a pretty wonderful experience, though it could also break your heart. My classmate and I had totally different views of Johnny Nolan: he thought he was *nothing but* an alcoholic, I thought he also was an extremely attractive, lovable person. Johnny's daughter, who has begun to see what a serious problem her father has, asks a provocative question of her teacher who has quoted Keats: "Beauty is truth, truth is beauty,—that is all we know on earth, and all we need to know." She says to the teacher, "If someone knew that and maybe was not so good at other things, it would be all right, wouldn't it?" Though the teacher dismisses the daughter's question, I cannot. The question again interests me since reading *Charming Billy.* The romantics, the poets and the dreamers are onto something very important. I am grateful for those I've met in life and in literature.

One of the priests in the group discussing *Charming Billy* mentioned during the discussion that there was no character in the book that was not likable. He asked the group, "Why is that?" He thought it was because of their faith. If he is correct, and I think he is, this strengthens the interpretation of the novel which sees *Charming Billy* as being about the communion of saints.

A Contemporary Parable

In 1999 the gifted Catholic author Andre Dubus died. Back in 1986 Dubus had been hit by a car when he tried to be a good Samaritan by helping two stranded motorists on a highway. In fact, it is possible that Andre saved one of the motorists' lives by pushing her away from an oncoming vehicle. The price of his heroism was that both of his legs were crushed. One leg was eventually amputated and Andre was to spend the rest of his life in a wheelchair. Writing in *America* magazine (March 20, 2001), Patrick Samway, S.J., tells of a visit he had with his friend, Dubus, back in August of 1986. Samway reports that though Dubus understandably reached bottom after his accident, Andre struggled against destructive self-pity and eventually called his experience of suffering, of being a cripple, a gift from God. Dubus writes that his experience of suffering was like being grabbed by his guardian angel and pulled up a little higher. Dubus must have been quite a man!

Dubus had a sacramental view of reality. One of his short stories, "A Father's Story" is exceptionally powerful and, like one of Jesus' parables, moves us to think about God the Father's love for us. In the story Dubus created a character, Luke Ripley, whose love for his daughter goes beyond just about everything else in his life. After his daughter, inadvertently, late at night, hits a man with a car, Luke goes out and discovers that the man is dead but he does not tell anyone about the incident, neither the police nor the parish priest, who is his confessor and best friend. Dubus depicts Luke, a daily communicant, having dialogue with God. After Luke tells God that the deception he did for his daughter he would not have done for his sons, the following dialogue ensues:

"Why? Do you love them less?'

'I tell Him no, it is not that I love them less, but that I could bear the pain of watching and knowing my sons' pain, could bear it with pride as they took the whip and nails. 'But You never had a daughter and, if You had, You could not have borne her passion.'

'So,' He says, 'You love her more than you love Me.'

'I love her more than I love truth.'

'Then you love in weakness,' He says.

'As you love me,' I say." [13]

In *Commonweal* Father John Breslin, S.J. wrote a marvelous tribute to Dubus:

"Perhaps Dubus' greatest contribution to contemporary writing was his enormous compassion. You cannot read his stories without feeling his commitment to his characters, even the thieves and the rapists. Dubus took the Jesus of the parables at face value, and nowhere more so than in his refusal to play judge. With the biblical Jeremiah, he affirmed the tortuousness of the human heart, its endless complexity and complicity. But the ultimate source of Dubus' compassion was his faith in a God as close as the next moment of silence or the bread and wine on the altar. When Luke Ripley rejoices that after 48 years he still feels excitement on receiving the host at Mass, we do no violence to the story to hear the authentic tones of Dubus' own voice. We shall miss him." [14]

Great literature can seduce us. It can awaken us and call us to enter more deeply into relationship with others and with God.

Questions for Reflection

1. Do you think of Mass as a narrative? If so, how is it narrative?

2. What kind of truth is in fiction that is different from the truth in history?

3. Do you think Scobie is a saint? Why or why not?

4. Why or why not is the "whiskey priest" in *The Power and the Glory* a saint?

5. Is "The Trouble" anti-Catholic? Why or why not?

6. Would "The Hint of an Explanation" help or hinder people's understanding of the Eucharist?

7. In relation to film, theater and especially literature, can you think of evidence to support Brother Michel's claim that ours is a "post-Christian age"?

8. According to Bernard Lonergan what is an intellectual conversion? A moral conversion? A religious conversion?

9. Do you think Alice McDermott's *Charming Billy* is about faith? Is Billy holy?

10. In "A Father's Story" is the human father like God the Father? In what ways "yes" and in what ways "no"?

[1] Flannery O'Connor, *Mystery and Manners* (New York: Farrar, Straus & Giroux, 1957), p. 153.

[2] Ron Hansen, *A Stay Against Confusion: Essays on Faith and Fiction* (New York: Harper Collins, 2001), p. 11.

[3] Evelyn Waugh in *Commonweal Confronts the Century: Liberal Convictions, Catholic Traditions* with an Introduction by Peter Steinfels, edited by Patrick K. Jordan and Paul Baumann (New York: a Touchstone Book, Simon and Schuster, 1999), p. 380.

[4] Graham Greene, *The Heart of the Matter* (New York: Penguin Books, 1948), p.272.

[5] Brother Michel Bettigole, OSF, *Tales of God: A Treasury of Great Short Stories for the Catholic Family* (New York: Alba House, 2001), p. IX.

[6] Graham Greene, "The Hint of an Explanation" in *Tales of God: A Treasury of Great Short Stories for the Catholic Family,* op. cit., pp. 183-184.

[7] Brother Michel Bettigole, OSF, *op. cit.,* p. IX.

[8] Ibid., pp. IX-X.

[9] Richard Gilman, *Faith, Sex and Mystery* (New York: Simon and Schuster, 1986), pp. 49-53.

[10] Flannery O'Connor, *op. cit.*

[11] Ibid., p. 150.

[12] Alice McDermott, *Charming Billy* (New York: Farrar, Straus & Giroux, 1998), pp. 235-236.

[13] Andre Dubus, "A Father's Story" in *The Substance of Things Hoped For, Short Fiction by Modern Catholic Authors,* selected with an introduction by John B. Breslin, S.J. (Garden City, New York: Doubleday & Company, 1987), pp. 166-167.

[14] John Breslin, S.J. , "Andre Dubus, R.I.P.", in *Commonweal,* April 23, 1999, p. 11.

5

The Magnetism of Painting

*"The artist is a sacrament maker, a creator of emphasized,
clarified beauty designed to make us see. If grace is everywhere, it is superabundant in the world of art. . . ."* [1]

—Andrew Greeley

Occasionally in philosophy classes at St. John's
University when I am lecturing on an especially mysteri-
ous truth about God or about the human person I attempt
a humorous remark such as "Would any one else in the
class care to say something because I don't know what I
am talking about?" It usually gets a chuckle. When I write
about painting, I feel I ought to preface my remarks with
a confession of my ignorance about painting. In discussing painting I am an interested neophyte.

Recently I was recalling the excitement in my family
when, many years ago, we received our first television set.
That was in the late 1940s. At that time there was not
much on television that today we would think of as exciting. The two most famous shows were Milton Berle's
"Texaco Star Theater" on Tuesday evenings and Ed
Sullivan's show, then called "The Toast of the Town," on
Sunday evenings. Berle and Sullivan brought famous
stars of stage and screen into our living rooms.

In those days the possibilities of television seemed unlimited. What could not be brought into our living rooms? Television could cause a revolution in education, we thought, as the world's great cultural achievements would appear on television sets throughout our country. It did not quite happen the way we imagined and I suppose the jury is still out on whether television has been a blessing or a bane. But at least occasionally something special does come along and those of us who now rarely if ever watch television have something to renew our hope. The series that Sister Wendy did on PBS, "Sister Wendy's Story of Painting," was something special. It was exceptionally good, both entertaining and educational. Originally ten hours in Britain, Sister Wendy's show was cut to five hours on PBS.

Over the last fifteen years or so I have been trying to improve on my art education by making five or six trips into Manhattan each year to visit either the Metropolitan Museum of Art or The Museum of Modern Art or the Frick Museum. From time to time I have been tempted to enroll in a course on art history at some school. As a professor of philosophy at St. John's University, I am always delighted to have pointed out to me the relations between the philosophy of a given period and the art of that period. I find it absolutely fascinating to see how the same idea appears in a philosopher's writing and on a painter's canvas. Indeed to see the relationships among painting, film, theater, philosophy, music, architecture and the literature of a given period can be quite exciting. Instead of me enrolling in a course, PBS and Sister Wendy brought the course into my room and onto my TV screen.

Sister Wendy is a 70-year-old Roman Catholic sister, who since 1970 has lived at a Carmelite monastery in Norfolk, England. She spent years studying art. I find her talent for finding a story in a painting especially intriguing. In the television series, as she narrates the story she finds in a work, the painting comes alive in a new way. Sister has the wonderful qualities of being both clear and profound in her comments. For example, in commenting on the art in the Lascaux caves, she noted the yearning of humankind "to be strong and beautiful, free, innocent, all the things that they were not and we are not."

Her enthusiasm is infectious. If I were not interested in painting, I suspect that listening to Sister Wendy would convert me. After listening to her comments on a painting, I become aware that she has seen in the painting much more than I would ever see without her guidance but in addition to her knowledge, I greatly appreciate her excitement. What she is doing is obviously a labor of love and her excitement comes right through the screen and motivates me to try to further appreciate the world's masterpieces.

One show that I viewed dealt with paintings in Florence. Viewing the show I recalled vividly my experience of the city. In Florence, I came to understand what people mean when they talk about a city being beautiful. Not everyone can go to Florence but through Sister Wendy and PBS at least something of the beauty of Florence's treasures has been made available.

Not surprisingly, Sister Wendy's comments often include a moral message. I find this especially interesting. It seems to me that Sister Wendy is combining her knowledge of art with her knowledge of human nature and the blend of the two is quite appealing.

Technically, the series was excellent. There is no substitute for actually being physically present to the great works of art but through very fine camera work, color and music, the series provided the next best thing to actual physical presence. With such an outstanding series television at least occasionally fulfills its potential.

Shortly after the five-part series had appeared Sister Wendy was interviewed by Bill Moyers on PBS. It was the best interview I have ever seen on television. Several things about the interview greatly impressed me. I was struck by the apparent ease with which Sister Wendy answered questions. While Bill Moyers had notes, she did not and yet she never stumbled, though some of the questions were quite difficult. I was also struck by her honesty and ability to speak unselfconsciously about her own life. She confessed that prior to her own show, she had never watched television. To me this made both her lectures about painting and the interview even more amazing.

When asked about her life, Sister said that she spends a great deal of time praying. Explaining why she wears the traditional habit, she said that as a contemplative sister, she looks upon the habit as a practical convenience. Wearing it frees her from the daily decisions about what to wear and so she is not distracted from thinking about God.

She described her vocation as a contemplative sister as "living in the sunshine of God's presence" and that this was "absolute bliss." Though she believes that her lecturing on television about art is an important service, she

said that she will welcome leaving the world of celebrity
and returning to the monastery. Especially touching was
the way that Sister spoke about her discovery of her own
vocation. Claiming that when she was 13, she knew that
she wanted to be a sister, she described herself as an inadequate woman, as somewhat cold emotionally. Viewing
her on television, I find that very difficult to believe. But
she said that sex never held any interest for her personally and though her parents were happily married, she
never had a desire to marry. In fact, she said that she only
came to understand some very basic facts about sex after
it was necessary for her as a sister to teach those facts to
others.

There was one other comment about a religious vocation that I found provocative. She said one sign of a vocation is that the person "needs it to be fully human." I don't
think I had ever heard a religious vocation spoken about
in exactly those terms. The idea fascinates me: that I could
not be fully I, that I could not reach the depth of being
human, without my vocation.

After seeing Sister Wendy's five-part series and watching the interview with Moyers, I went to see exhibits on
Monet and Degas. As I attended those two exhibits, I had
in mind some of the tips that Sister Wendy offered for
those of us who need guidance in viewing paintings. She
suggested that we should try for an unmediated reaction
to the work. In other words, do not approach the work
with some hidden agenda that you will impose on the
work, but rather go to the work defenseless and allow the
work to speak to you. She also suggested that it is good to
spend some time allowing your eyes to roam around the

painting. After doing that, it can be good to leave the painting, to walk away from it and return later. This will give you time to see and absorb what is there. Sister said that if we give the painting our attention and our time, eventually the work will begin to flow within us. She suggested that we surrender to the wonder of the story. For Sister, looking and waiting are the keys.

Art: A Help to Be More Spiritual

At one point in the interview, Bill Moyers asked Sister what art had done for her. I found her reflections on the power of art to free us especially interesting. She suggested that there is a great temptation to live as a zombie, to allow life to pass by without experiencing it fully. She said that art helps us to be alert, to be there, to be present.

Art demands attention and so it helps us to be more attentive. People can go around in a cage and art opens the cage. All art is spiritual and so art, said Sister Wendy, helps us to be more spiritual. I don't know whether I have ever heard a more accurate and yet more simple explanation of what art can do for us.

Beauty is fascinating. I can recall a visit to the Frick Museum in New York City with a friend and both of us were overwhelmed by the beauty in the Museum. I had been to the Frick several times. The first time I visited the Frick I was stunned by one room in particular. As I recall there were about thirty paintings in the room. It seemed as though each time I looked at a painting I thought it was one of the most beautiful paintings I had ever seen. I would move on to the next painting which I then thought was even more beautiful than the previous one I had been admiring. This continued to be my experience as I moved around the room. The beauty of the paintings contained within the walls of the room was awesome. How did artists succeed in capturing such beauty, in expressing such beauty?

The day my friend and I went to the Frick together we used the portable hearing device provided by the Museum. We listened to comments on more than thirty works of art. My friend, who had never been to the Museum, had a reaction similar to the one I had the first time I visited the Frick. My friend kept making statements such as "This is fantastic. This is incredible. I am coming back."

My friend and I spent about two hours at the Frick, two hours experiencing beauty. Our experience may or may not have been an experience of prayer but I think it was a deeply spiritual experience. In an exceptionally good article on beauty entitled "The Apologetics of Beauty," Father Andrew Greeley makes some very important points. He writes:

> "Humanly created beauty that does not seem explicitly religious can be religious insofar as it tricks us into enchantment and thus opens us up to the illuminations of Being—stopping us in our tracks, whether we want to be stopped in our tracks or not. The reconciliation arias at the end of the 'Marriage of Figaro', American folk songs like 'Shenandoah', a skyline viewed from a body of water in the moonlight, Seamus Heaney's love poem, 'The Otter,' Rilke's protest that he needs no more springtime because one is already too

much for his blood, the hope that ugliness and
terror cannot exorcise from a Stephen King
novel, Molly Bloom's celebration of life and love
at the end of Ulysses. If grace is everywhere, it is
superabundant in the world of art, when one is
open to seeing it."[2]

Is Father Greeley correct in saying that grace is superabundant in the world of art? I think he is in the sense that
art reveals beauty to us and Beauty ultimately is God.
When my friend and I went to the Frick neither of us
thought that we were doing a religious act. We were going
to see some beautiful works of art. But I think that Father
Greeley is correct in saying that humanly created beauty
can trick "us into enchantment" and "stop us in our
tracks." Jesuit poet Gerard Manley Hopkins was saying
something profoundly true when he wrote "The world is
charged with the grandeur of God." I confess that I am
often blind to that grandeur but that art sometimes opens
me up to it.

Film, theater, literature and painting can take us
beyond the everyday world, the world of routine and
open us up to the mystery of God. Great art is sacramental in the sense that it is a sign of the Mystery at the heart
of creation. The artist need not be a religious believer in
order to reveal the Mystery of God to us. Nor need the
work of art be obviously religious. The artist contemplates
the mystery of being and tries to express it to us in painting, sculpture, music, theater, film or literature and an
epiphany of God can take place.

It may be because American Catholics have tended to
be practical and pragmatic even in our understanding of

our faith that we have not seen the importance of art or appreciated the value and power of art. Perhaps art has seemed abstract to us or esoteric. That is unfortunate. Art that is beautiful can contribute greatly to our lives. Beautiful art can speak to us of God.

There were many beautiful paintings in an exhibit at the Metropolitan Museum of Art entitled "Manet/Velazquez: The French Taste for Spanish Painting." I believe that there are two aspects of every great painting that can contribute to the painting's beauty being a revelation of the beauty of God. One I would call the theme or the idea or the vision that the painting is revealing. The other I would call the manner in which the artist put his or her idea on the canvas. By the manner I would include the colors, the type of brush strokes, the lighting, the composition of figures and anything else that the artist uses to get what he or she is trying to say into the painting.

In a perceptive and illuminating essay in *The New York Times* entitled "The Masters of the French Masters Were Spanish," Michael Kimmelman includes some interesting anecdotes. He mentions a remark by the great painter Rubens which Kimmelman thinks is apocryphal. Believing himself to be the greatest painter alive, Rubens went to Madrid in the 1620s and met Velazquez. After looking at the Spanish painter's art Rubens supposedly said "Oh, I didn't know about him." Even if the incident never happened the story does give some sense of just how great an artist Velazquez was. Kimmelman reports that after Manet saw Velazquez's work the French painter said that he didn't know why anyone else bothered to paint.

What interests me most about painting and indeed about all art is what the artist is trying to say or communicate. Praising Velazquez's work Kimmelman ends his essay as follows:

"It seems to reach across the ages. The writer Ortega y Gasset said Velazquez's work isn't art; it is life perpetuated.

"I think something Lucian Freud once observed about Rembrandt describes the same effect. 'You feel you are privileged,' he said, 'because the artist is giving you an ennobling insight into the nature of people. I don't mean he has made the people seem virtuous, but I mean it is ennobling to be told something so truthful.'

"Great art is always about human nature. This show is full of truths about life." [3]

It is because great art is about human nature that I think it is so interesting and so important. Great artists look at the beauty of God's creation and then can make that beauty more evident and accessible to us. Some of Velazquez's paintings are breathtakingly beautiful. I marvel at his talent and skill, at his greatness.

In reflecting on beauty I have been helped by John Haught's book *What is God? How to Think About the Divine.* In discussing beauty Haught writes the following:

"Alfred North Whitehead, whose philosophy is permeated by aesthetic considerations, tells us that beauty is the 'harmony of contrasts.' What makes us appreciate the beauty of things is that they bring together nuance, richness, complexity and novelty on the one side, and harmony, pattern or order on the other. The more 'intense' the synthesis of harmony and contrast, the more we appreciate their union. Nuance without harmony is chaos, and harmony without nuance is monotony. Beauty involves the transformation of potentially clashing elements into pleasing contrasts harmonized by the overarching aesthetic pattern of the beautiful object or experience."[4]

Whitehead's insights into beauty are obvious to me in relation to literature, film and theater. I think his theory of aesthetics works with those three arts and I suspect it works with painting also.

I think that some artists, and I include among this group some playwrights, novelists, and filmmakers, have substituted art for religion. Though I don't agree with them I think we should never underestimate the power of art to influence us and illuminate for us some of life's mysteries. It is easy to dismiss art that is new and unconventional and I am often tempted to do that. But we should be open to meaning and mystery wherever we find it.

Whenever I go to an art museum I find myself especially attracted to religious paintings. There are probably several reasons for this. One is my interest in religion. Another is that I find religious paintings easier to understand and appreciate. A third reason is that I am fascinated by how artists, and I mean all artists, not just painters, try to depict the supernatural or the mystery of God's presence. How does a novelist or a filmmaker or a poet or a sculptor or a playwright capture the presence of God in his or her work? In film today, because of technology, it is relatively easy to depict a physical miracle such as the parting of the Red Sea but not so easy to depict the presence of grace.

There is a religious painting at the Frick Museum which the Museum audiotape described as the greatest Renaissance painting in this country. It is "St. Francis in the Desert" by Giovanni Bellini (c. 1430-1516). It is magnificent, and it alone warrants a trip to the Frick. Bellini portrays Francis in ecstasy, and the stigmata are evident on the saint's hands. Standing by the side of a mountain, the saint, with his hands spread out at his sides, apparently is having a vision. He is looking at something other than what is depicted in the painting. The city is seen off in the distance as is a gorgeous blue sky peppered with fluffy white clouds. As I viewed the painting, I tried to follow the advice of Sister Wendy and allow the painting "to wash over me." Of course Bellini did not attempt to paint God, but he did successfully create a beautiful painting that depicts God's impact on a great saint.

In Father Greeley's essay on beauty he writes:

"Human artists see things more clearly than the rest of us. They penetrate into the illumination of being more intimately than do the rest of us. They want us to see what they see so that we can share in their illumination. They are driven to duplicate that beauty in their work... The artist is a sacrament maker, a creator of emphasized, clarified beauty designed to make us see. Artists invite us into the world they see so that we can go forth from that world enchanted by the luminosity of their work and with enhanced awareness of the possibilities of life." [5]

I agree completely with Greeley's observations. Artists see what the rest of us miss. I recall team-teaching a film course with a priest-artist thirty years ago. We would view films together in preparing our class lectures. I was amazed at what he saw on the screen that I missed. His "eye" was much more sensitive than mine to many of the visual details which conveyed the meaning of the film. Giving the course with him was an education for me.

I do believe that artists penetrate more deeply into the illumination of being than do the rest of us. Great art can open us up to the meaning and mystery of the human and the meaning and mystery of the divine. All of us should be grateful that artists share what they see with the rest of us. A priest friend of mine once told me that he thought all artists should go straight to heaven because they have given so much to people.

Artists are makers of sacraments in the sense that they use signs and symbols to portray mystery. If we see what they want us to see, then we really can be transformed by works of art. Artists are gift-givers and the gifts they give are important if we are going to develop as human beings. I think of art that has touched me deeply, films, plays, novels and paintings that have had a deep impact on me. Some works of art have affected me on the conscious level, some on a level that I cannot clearly articulate. My life would be very different without the great art that I have experienced. My understanding of self and other would be dramatically different. My basic response to artists is one of gratitude.

Once I made a trip to the Metropolitan Museum to see an exhibit of the works of the great poet, William

Blake (1757-1827). I am embarrassed to admit that before I heard about the exhibit I did not even know that the great poet had done paintings. What made the exhibit especially attractive to me even before I saw it was the watercolor that the museum was using to advertise the show. The work is called "Angel of Revelation." Strikingly attractive, the watercolor conveys so much power that I can imagine viewers spontaneously stepping back when they first see it. Blake pictures St. John as a small figure sitting beneath a gigantic angel, who is portrayed as a physically strong man, towering over the evangelist. John is looking up at the angel.

I had heard Blake referred to as a mystic and so the idea of a mystic trying to depict in a watercolor the experience of a saint fascinated me. Seeing the exhibit and listening to the audio cassette that could be used as a companion, I learned that considering Blake as a mystic is just one interpretation of the poet-artist. Another interpretation of his work claims that Blake's "visions" can be explained through psychology. There is no way that anyone, least of all I, could prove which interpretation is correct. I prefer to think of Blake as a mystic because it makes his work more interesting to me.

By a mystic, I mean someone who has a deep experience of God that goes beyond ideas or concepts and that cannot be adequately expressed in words. Mystics sometimes are able to experience the presence of God in God's creatures. I think of the view of the Jewish personalist philosopher and religious thinker, Martin Buber, that creatures are like messages from God, words from God, and that if we are really present to creatures, we will become aware of God speaking to us.

Thinking of Blake as a mystic I recently re-read his beautiful poem "The Lamb." Whether Blake was or was not a mystic, I think of him as experiencing God in all things and then the poem takes on a deeper meaning for me. The following are a few lines from the poem:

> Little Lamb, who made thee?
> Dost thou know who made thee?
> Gave thee life & bid thee feed.
> By the stream & o'er the mead;
> Gave thee clothing of delight,
> Softest clothing, wooly, bright;
> ....
> He is called by thy name,
> For He calls himself a Lamb:
> He is meek, & he is mild;
> He became a little child.
> I a child, & thou a Lamb,
> We are called by his name.
> Little Lamb, God bless thee.
> Little Lamb, God bless thee.[6]

If I think of Blake as a mystic then I picture him experiencing the meaning of both creation and redemption in the lamb. All important meanings are revealed to Blake in his experience of the lamb.

The Surrealist Vision

A few years ago I attended an art exhibit devoted to Surrealism. My reaction was mixed. I first became interested in Surrealism through the films of Luis Buñuel. Back in the 1960s when I began taking film seriously, Buñuel along with Ingmar Bergman, Federico Fellini and Michelangelo Antonioni, were the giants whose films helped me to become aware that movies, which I had thought of as a pleasant diversion, were clearly a significant art form.

I have a vivid recollection of the first time I saw the short film by Buñuel and Salvador Dalí, "The Andalusian Dog" (1928). The film was written and directed by both Buñuel and Dalí. There is a scene in it from which I had to turn away. In the scene Buñuel is seated on a balcony looking up at the moon. A thin cloud is moving toward the moon. First, we see Buñuel's eyes looking up at the moon and then we see the thin cloud moving toward the moon. As the cloud moves toward the moon, a person with a straight razor stands behind Buñuel. As the cloud seems to cut through the moon, the person uses the razor to cut Buñuel's eye. Even though I knew I was watching a trick on film, the scene was so disturbing that I turned away.

That disturbance was exactly what Buñuel and Dalí desired. The point of the scene is that this film will "cut open" the eyes of the viewers and enable them to see what they would not ordinarily see. This is what surrealism is trying to do: enable us to see what we ordinarily do not see. Surrealism wants us to see what lies beneath and behind what we ordinarily call "reality." I certainly did not come away from the exhibit feeling that I had a comprehensive view of Surrealism but I did come away wishing that I understood Surrealism better. It was possible to leave the exhibit at different points to enter rooms in which works other than Surrealist were present. I walked into one such room and viewed paintings by Cezanne, Monet, Latrec, Renoir, Gaughin and Picasso. The contrast between these works and Surrealist art was striking. I really felt as though I had left one world and entered another.

There was no Surrealist work that I saw that I would describe as beautiful but I could describe almost all of them as interesting. Many of them seemed to be depictions of the unconscious, of hidden desires, dreams and wishes. Most of the paintings in the exhibit conveyed a kind of dream atmosphere. I don't think any of the paintings could be described as religious. Certainly I need to be educated before I will be able to appreciate in any depth just what Surrealism tries to do but the subconscious and the unconscious, just as every other part of human nature, are suitable areas for artists to explore. The mystery of the human person is unfathomable.

The Human Face of God

About as different from Surrealism as possible is the film *The Face: Jesus in Art*. Each Christian has his or her own image of Jesus. What most artists try to do when they depict Jesus is not so much strive for complete accuracy concerning his facial characteristics as try to capture something of the mystery of Jesus. Though they may not say this explicitly, when many artists depict a human face they are trying to capture something of the human mystery. When painting a human face, the artist may be able to convey some truth about a person's soul. What a challenge to try to depict the face of the Incarnate God! What a challenge to depict the invisible that became visible! "The Face: Jesus in Art" is like a mini-course in religious art.

Sponsored by the U.S. Bishops' Catholic Communication Campaign, the Dolan Family Foundation, Family Theater Productions, Our Sunday Visitor, United Methodist Communications and the Aztec Foundation, the film is narrated by actors such as Mel Gibson, Ricardo Montalban, Edward Herrmann, Stacy Keach, Patricia Neal and Juliette Mills. The performers who narrate the text are excellent, as is the text. Not only is the text interesting in its treatment of art but it is quite sound and in some sections theologically profound. The narrators give the impression that they are not really performing as much as expressing their own faith. But what is most marvelous in the film are the visuals. I confess that before I saw the film on video I had some misgivings about it. Wondering about how the film could avoid being static and dry, I pictured it as a kind of tour through the museums of the world. Thinking that the film might be interesting in terms of art history, I doubted that it could be very good as a film or movie because I could not imagine how it could be a dynamic, much less a fast moving, tour of art about Christ. I could not have been more wrong. The film is an artistic masterpiece. I am not exaggerating when I claim that it is thrilling. Possible descriptions that come to mind are "beautiful," "dazzling," "breathtaking" and "awesome."

I suppose what most impresses me about *The Face* is the camera work. Not only did the creators of the film weave together absolutely gorgeous shots of artistic masterpieces but they used the best contemporary technology to highlight the beauty of those masterpieces. At times—and I do not understand the technology that was used—the works of art seem to come to life and move. This film could well be a special opportunity to encounter Jesus Christ.

This chapter, indeed this entire book, is about seeing the face of Jesus. God speaks and is revealed to us in many ways and film, literature, theater and painting are among these ways. We are magnetized by God and the goal on this earth is an intimate relationship with God. We are being called by God. That call can come through film, theater, literature and painting.

Questions for Reflection

1. How is the artist a "sacrament maker"?
2. Do you have any favorite paintings? Do you think of them as religious?
3. How can art help us to be more spiritual?
4. How is grace superabundant in the world of art?
5. Is it true that "Great art is about humanity"?
6. Do you agree with what John Haught, relying on Alfred Whitehead, says about beauty? Is beauty "a harmony of contrasts"?
7. Can art enhance "our awareness of the possibilities of life" as Father Greeley claims?
8. Is Surrealism telling us something important about ourselves? Is it myopic? Trivial? Profound?
9. Is it true that all art—film, theater, literature and painting—is trying to depict the "face of God"? Explain your response to the question?

[1] Father Andrew Greeley, "The Apologetics of Beauty", *America*, September 16, 2000, p. 11.

[2] Ibid.

[3] Michael Kimmelman, "The Masters of the French Masters Were Spanish," *The New York. Times*, Online Edition, March 7, 2003, p. 5.

[4] John Haught, *What is God? How to Think About the Divine* (New York: Paulist Press, 1986), p. 72.

[5] Father Andrew Greeley, *op. cit.*, p. 11.

[6] William Blake, *The Complete Poetry and Prose*, edited by David V. Erdman, commentary by Harold Bloom (New York: Doubleday, an Anchor Book, 1988), pp. 8-9.

Conclusion

Our journey through life is a journey in which we are called to a deeper knowledge of self, neighbor and God. It is a journey also in which we are called to a deeper love of self, neighbor and God. There are many realities that can aid us in our journey. Parents, friends, schools and especially the Christian community help us on our journey toward deeper knowledge and toward a more profound life of love.

This book was written because of my belief that art can also help us on our journey through life. In my own life I have found film, theater, literature and painting a channel of God's Revelation. While I would not say that an aesthetic experience is the same as a religious experience, I am uncomfortable with a view that separates them too greatly. My hope is that these reflections help readers to be more attentive and more open to the treasures of film, theater, literature and art. As they encounter these forms of art, they may find, as in the rest of creation, God is reaching out to encounter them. They may discover they are magnetized by God.

Question for Reflection

1. Can you explain the title of this book?

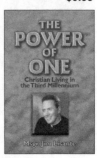